on track ...
Bob Dylan
1962 – 1970

Opher Goodwin

sonicbondpublishing.com

Sonicbond Publishing Limited
www.sonicbondpublishing.co.uk
Email: info@sonicbondpublishing.co.uk

First Published in the United Kingdom 2023
First Published in the United States 2023

British Library Cataloguing in Publication Data:
A Catalogue record for this book is available from the British Library

Copyright Opher Goodwin 2023

ISBN 978-1-78952-275-4

Typeset in ITC Garamond Std & ITC Avant Garde Gothic Pro
Printed and bound in England
Graphic design and typesetting: Full Moon Media

Follow us on social media:
Twitter: https://twitter.com/SonicbondP
Instagram: https://www.instagram.com/sonicbondpublishing_/
Facebook: https://www.facebook.com/SonicbondPublishing/

Linktree QR code:

on track ...

Bob Dylan 1962 – 1970

Contents

The highest purpose of art is to inspire. What else can you do for anyone but inspire them?

I'm an artist. I try to create art.

I'm sure of my dream self. I live in my dreams. I don't really live in the actual world.

I'll let you be in my dreams if I can be in yours.

I can't help what other people do with my songs, what they make of them.

Here lies Bob Dylan, murdered from behind by trembling flesh.

Love will conquer everything – I suppose.

Bob Dylan.

A man writes to throw off the poison which he has accumulated because of his false way of life. He is trying to recapture his innocence, yet all he succeeds in doing is to inoculate the world with a virus of his disillusionment.

Henry Miller.

Introduction

In 1962, at the age of thirteen, I was fortunate to be introduced to Bob
Dylan's music – though I did not fully appreciate that at the time. What
I could not see was that this raw 'folk' singer would become the fulcrum
around which rock music turned. I could not foresee that this intense ragged
acoustic oddity would soon weld depth and intelligence to visceral rebellion
to change the shape of pop music. From that first album, it was impossible
to understand that he would pave the way for the likes of Bobby Vee's two-
and-a-half-minute pop ditty 'Take Good Care of My Baby' to evolve into Roy
Harper's 20-minute poetic epic 'The Lord's Prayer'; that he would inspire
The Beatles to move from teeny-bop 'Love Me Do' to the surreal poetry and
experimentation of 'Strawberry Fields Forever'. But that's what he did.

A good friend of mine by the name of Charlie Mutton had purchased Bob's
debut album shortly after it was released and he was smitten. That was
peculiar. Up to that time, we had been listening to chart material and old
rock 'n' roll. Heaven knows where Mutt picked up on Dylan's first album.
I don't remember it being either popular or available in my neck of the
woods. We weren't big on 'folk' music. However, my ears weren't tuned
in to the raw, nasally sound of Bob's folk blues and, although I listened all
the way through and even appreciated a number of the tracks, I was not
greatly impressed. Mutt was more clued up and assured me that Dylan was
going to be huge and if he'd only release a single, it would be a top-ten hit. I
remained quietly sceptical.

Mutt was incredibly prophetic. Subsequent albums and the 'Times They
Are A-Changin'' single did just as he had predicted. Bob Dylan went on to
become one of the most important figures in the history of rock music. Not
only did he change the face of rock music, but he also had a profound effect
on the direction of youth culture. Once I'd 'got it', and my ears became more
accustomed, I, too, was utterly smitten.

As with Dylan, I was caught up in the zeitgeist of the time. These were
the days of great divisions in society: a rising rebellious youth, the threat of
instant annihilation from nuclear war and dramatic changes in attitudes. The
traumas of the second world war were still fresh, but the economy and world
were opening up. Change was in the air. Our parents represented something
we did not want to be. Bob was riding that wave of change.

The 1950s Beats may have cracked the façade of the rigid conformity and
strict hypocritical morality of the prevailing post-war 1950s culture. Rock 'n'
roll and r&b may have liberated youth into a temporary hedonistic frenzy,
but it was the 1960s generation who blew the whole structure to smithereens.
Peculiarly, Robert Zimmerman found himself, sometimes unwillingly, right at
the forefront of those shifts in the tectonic plates of society. Who could have
predicted that? Who could have known that this young middle-class Jewish
kid from a decaying nondescript town in the middle of nowhere would create
a persona and develop the skills to take the whole world by storm?

That early Dylan was a chameleon, a sponge, a mirror, a driven force, who was searching for identity, acceptance and fame. He absorbed everything around him with an unquenchable thirst, then reflected it back a hundred times brighter. He took on his surroundings and magnified them. For that young Dylan, integrity was all that counted. Authenticity and cool were the only important things. Robert Zimmerman was an empty vessel into which he poured the ingredients that created Bob Dylan. That early incarnation was a wild vortex of possibility. He manufactured a persona and mythology on which to hang the brilliance of his craft. Everything about Bob Dylan was false, a construct, apart from his natural talent. His persona was nothing more than a vehicle to transport him to where he wanted to go. Young Bob Dylan was ruthless. He drained everyone around him dry, wringing out their songs, their chords, their tunes, friendships and love. I'm not implying that this was intentional or, in any way mean, merely necessary. In order to get to where he needed to be, he had to grow, blossom and change. Nothing was more important. Bob was helplessly riding a tsunami that he himself created. At times, for the people involved – Suze Rotolo, Joan Baez, Phil Ochs, Martin Carthy and Dave Van Ronk, to name a few – it must have felt as if they were being used and abused.

That fledgling Dylan (Robert Allen Zimmerman) was on a roller-coaster that kept changing tracks. Seemingly, he had no compunctions about leaving people and whole movements behind. Parents, lovers, friends and fellow musicians bit the dust. He moved on when the need arose, without scruples and ne'er a backward glance. The chameleon had to grow and move. That was his nature, all he knew. The biographies are numerous, the details mauled over, magnified, twisted, sensationalised and made to fit the required template. Hard to disentangle reality from myth. There lived a legend largely generated by Bob himself in his quest to create credibility and breakthrough. Life for a musician was cutthroat. Most fell by the wayside. Talent was not the only criterion necessary; having the correct image, credentials, friends, disposition, drive and luck was also a necessity. What Robert Allan Zimmerman lacked he created for himself out of thin air.

Looking back to the early John Bucklen tapes – recorded in 1958 on a portable reel-to-reel tape recorder – of a young Robert Zimmerman, seventeen years old, still at school, pounding out his homage to his idol Little Richard, there was no inkling of the folk legend he was shortly to become. He wanted to become a rock star. That teenage Dylan was a rebel, assuming an image based on James Dean and Marlon Brando. He formed several loud rock 'n' roll bands, the Golden Chords and Shadow Blasters being two, in which he pounded the piano oblivious to audience response. In the first of his chameleonic changes, he assumed the name and wild persona of Elston Gunn. Despite his naked enthusiasm, the bands didn't take off – they had nowhere to go – but they did bring him some local notoriety and attract the girls. He was very much into girls and rock music was both a magnet and an aphrodisiac. A big motivator. This increasing rebelliousness led to fractious relationships with school, the tight-knit Jewish community and his father.

By the age of eighteen, he'd wrung the little Minnesotan iron ore town of Hibbing dry. He'd learnt the rudiments of guitar and piano, formed several bands, and absorbed a huge range of musical styles and traditions from rock 'n' roll, r&b, country music and standards – the mainstay of the local radio station, all of which were going to contribute and inform his progressions over the course of the ensuing years. Groundwork was being laid. Bob's tastes were eclectic – his first musical heroes being Hank Williams and Little Richard.

Here we must begin to unravel the man from the myth. Robert Zimmerman was already outgrowing the little mining town of Hibbing in Minnesota. As soon as he was able, he looked for a way out of there. A fresh-faced boy, looking younger than his years, not yet needing to shave, set off on the start of his adventure.

He did not exactly run away from home as seek out an excuse to leave. No, he hadn't already absconded from home seven times (at the age of ten, twelve, thirteen, fifteen, fifteen and a half, seventeen and eighteen). No, he hadn't spent six years with a travelling carnival. No, he hadn't ridden the freights as a hobo from Gallop, New Mexico, to New Orleans. No, he wasn't an orphan. It was all much less colourful than that. He'd been brought up in a Jewish family with a middle-class upbringing and led a rather uneventful life in a small town, but he was obsessed with music and determined to have a life in music. Apart from girls, it was all he cared about. Remarkably, as a young kid, he managed to secure a gig or three backing Bobby Vee on the piano when he'd appeared in the local area. That must have been a real buzz. In 1959, looking for a way of getting into the music business, he persuaded his mother to help him out. Using a course at Minnesota University as an excuse to leave Hibbing, he gained the help of his mother (his relationship with his more conservative father being difficult). She arranged for him to go to Minnesota by organising with his cousin Chucky to put him up. Chucky sorted him a room in the frat house at the university where he could stay for free in the summer. Not exactly as exciting as riding freights and touring with carnivals, but it did set him on the road. Upon arriving on the greyhound bus, he immediately swapped his electric guitar for an acoustic Martin Double O so that he could set about playing in the local coffee houses. It was the start. What he did next was to seek out like-minded people, hang out with musicians, and have the time to develop, learn and evolve. The liberal arts course at the University of Minnesota was not scintillating enough. Bob focused more on his music, staying up late to play, listen, drink and party. For the young Robert, girls, dope and booze were more interesting than studying and he soon dropped out.

As soon as he reached Minnesota, he left behind the image of Elston Gunnn, abandoned rock 'n' roll, took up the acoustic guitar and came under the spell of a new genre. His introduction to folk was Odetta: 'The first thing that turned me on to folk was Odetta – something vital and personal.' Later he discovered a new master; Woody Guthrie loomed like a giant on the scene. He was introduced to Woody by Flo Castner, a wacky actress and waitress. On first hearing the songs, his head was spinning: 'It was like the land parted'. The young eighteen-year-old Bobby was completely blown away. He hadn't heard anything like it before. Woody songs were 'All I wanted to sing'. Years later, he wrote in his biography *Chronicles*: 'I had been in the dark and someone turned on the main switch of a lightning conductor.' Zimmerman immersed himself in the burgeoning folk-blues scene and the social commentary of Woody Guthrie.

Bob settled into life in Minnesota, living hand to mouth, playing the coffee bars where baskets were passed around for change. This was the start of his freewheelin' days; cadging meals, renting a small apartment, sleeping on friends' floors, playing music, listening, absorbing and developing fast.

Minnesota wasn't big enough. He instinctively craved a bigger canvas and had heard that Woody was still alive but suffering from a chronic illness, the dreadful hereditary disease Huntingdon's Chorea, and holed up in a sanatorium in New Jersey. There was only one place to be, where the remains of the Beat movement had morphed into a vibrant underground folk scene, and that was Greenwich Village in New York. However, this young man, pretending to be the wild maverick, still had to persuade his father to allow him to drop out and give it a try. His father grudgingly agreed to allow him a year in which to make it.

In 1961, at the age of 20, still looking like a young kid, a nascent Bob Dylan rolled into town, not on a freight, but having secured a lift in an old Buick. Stepping out into the icy blast of a New York winter, Bob had little apart from a bag containing all his possessions and a guitar. He had two major aims: to meet his new idol Woody Guthrie and to break into the thriving new Folk scene. He set about finding a café to play in with a warm place to crash down and get out of the cold. He found it at The Café Wha?. He was allowed to back Fred Neil on harmonica and play the odd set which gave him somewhere to escape the cruel wind while earning a dollar or two and filling his stomach with a greasy burger. The Café Wha? Provided him with a base to learn and grow.

The Greenwich Village scene was based around several small clubs and overrun with a range of musicians all competing for time, money and status – pretty cutthroat. The musicians ranged from old well-versed blues musicians like John Lee Hooker, Jimmy Reed, Jesse Fuller and Big Bill Broonzy, seasoned folk singers, Woody Guthrie acolytes, like Ramblin' Jack Elliott, Pete Seeger and Cisco Houston, folk groups like the Bluegrass Boys, Clancy Brothers and the new generation of up-and-coming singers Tom Paxton, Mark Spoeltra, Odetta and Richard Farina. The leading light was Dave Van Ronk, a powerful figure, nicknamed 'The Mayor' who presided over the whole scene like a brooding grizzly bear.

No naive middle-class novice was going to stand a chance of breaking through into that environment. Robert Zimmerman from Hibbing morphed into Bob Dylan. He intended to drop the Zimmerman and become Bob Allen but thought that Dylan sounded better than Allen, so he adapted it – not so much stealing his name from a notorious Welsh poet as simply preferring the sound of Dylan to Allen. Having a new name, he set about creating a hard-living mythology – an orphaned past, running away numerous times, life on the road, carnivals, and hard times. Bob was constructing a suitable persona and appearance. The black corduroy cap, crumpled shirt, jeans, belt and boots were a carefully choreographed image. There had to be no chink in the armour. From the nasally Woody-esque drawl to the embroidered back story, the whole package had to hang together. Dylan grew into the disguise. What helped was the huge natural talent that Bob was so obviously saturated with.

His act involved Chaplin-esque routines, carefully orchestrated ploys, tuning and fiddling with his guitar and harmonica, all with casual glances and asides, designed to draw the audience in. From the very start, it was apparent that Bob, despite his shyness and boyish looks, possessed a great stage presence. Not only that, but he was already beginning to write his own material and what songs they were!

There were a large number of factors that fed into this burgeoning songwriting. The exposure to a wide range of music – being able to watch, at close hand, experienced musicians applying their stage skills (most of whom recognised his talent and encouraged him), the befriending of Dave Van Ronk, who carried huge clout, and his love affair with Suze Rotolo. This young Dylan was avidly listening to a range of music, reading poetry and literature, ransacking the libraries and record collections of all and sundry.

Suze was hugely instrumental in the development of his social sensitivities and outlook. She came from a dyed-in-the-wool communist family and already, as a young girl, had been involved in the civil rights movement.

The early sixties were the time of civil rights, the bomb, the cold war and the beginnings of the war in Vietnam. This was the McCarthy era with its hounding of communists and unAmerican activities. The Beat generation had instigated dissent and now the folk scene, mainly due to Woody Guthrie and Pete Seeger, was the seat of left-wing social change, a movement that was going to blossom and shape the whole sixties underground movement. Suze was steeped in it. Bob absorbed it so that it permeated much of his writing.

Between 1961 and 1963, prompted by Suze and the folk scene in general, Dylan wrote many of his most famous socially motivated songs, songs that laid the groundwork for the sixties philosophy. His wordmanship was constantly developing and reaching new heights. Unfortunately, it saddled Dylan with being the voice of a generation, an epithet loaded on him by the media that not only irritated him no end but one which heaped tension on his shoulders.

With his manager – the great behemoth Albert Grossman, a recording contract with Colombia Records, his adoption by Joan Baez and promotion through Pete Seeger, Bob Dylan set off on a meteoric trajectory to become a massive international star and in so doing, boosted folk music and poetic songwriting into another sphere. Inevitably, the result of such fame brought adulation, crowds of screaming fans, hangers-on and a need for safety and security that locked Bob into a bubble, away from his freewheelin' days around Greenwich Village.

After the breakdown of his relationship with Suze, maybe in response to being saddled with the limiting description of being a 'protest' singer, Bob moved away from writing songs of social import into writing songs of a more introspective nature influenced by the French symbolist poets Rimbaud, Baudelaire and Verlaine. Later, Dylan fell under the spell of the Beat poets, principally Allen Ginsberg, and began writing more complex surreal landscapes.

The 'folk period' had produced a fine debut album followed by three classic acoustic albums. Ironically, even as his fame peaked he was tiring of the limitations of his acoustic songs, feeling staid and dissatisfied. He felt everything was predictable and was on the verge of completely abandoning his career: 'I guess I was going to quit singing. I was drained. I was playing a lot of songs I did not want to play.' 'I was getting very bored with that.' 'It's very tiring having other people tell you how much they dig you if you yourself don't dig you.'

In 1964, The Beatles broke big in the USA and then the likes of The Byrds and Manfred Mann took rock 'n' roll versions of his songs into the charts. The Animals took the traditional 'House of the Rising Sun' to number one. It sparked something in Bob and rekindled his love of rock. He, with the help of the Paul Butterfield Blues Band and then The Hawks, later to become The Band, turned electric.

The move away from the 'authentic purity' of folk music coupled with the abandonment of what was seen as 'protest' created havoc. The folk music purists thought they had been betrayed. The corduroy cap and carefully cultivated scruffy attire bit the dust. A new incarnation was spawned. This period reflected Bob as the hipster, polka-dot, dark-sun-glassed rock star – the coolest dude on the planet. The changes gave birth to three ground-breaking albums of extraordinary depth and innovation but were not without great controversy. The live concerts featured a band with loud electric instruments eliciting shouts of 'Judas', much booing and a great split in his audience. Dylan treated the negative reactions with complete disdain – extolling his band to 'play fucking loud'. Dylan had moved on – all stoked up on amphetamines, mellowed out on hash and now dropping acid, egged on by his equally acerbic friend Bobby Neuwirth, surrounded by an entourage of minders, sycophants and hangers-on, overseen by emperor Albert Grossman, Bob held court with baffling, surreal interviews, caustic disembowelments of reporters or those who managed to penetrate his shield and an increasing helter-skelter of parties, concerts and travel. Life had become a circus in which he somehow managed to keep producing music and poetry of a superlative standard. Albert kept Bob's nose to the grindstone, milking the holy cow, signing contracts for books, albums and concert tours. The pressure never let up. As the carnival swirled around him, Dylan tapped away on his typewriter, trying to produce the novel *Tarantula* that he had committed himself to write, trying out new songs on guitar or piano, contemplating the endless stream of concerts and recording contracts that Albert had negotiated. Everything zipped by in a hyped-up, amphetamine-fuelled haze. Bob was permanently wired. The strain was beginning to tell. There seemed only one conclusion to this relentless pressure. Sure enough, it all came to a head.

While motorcycling around Woodstock, he had an accident in which he injured his neck. Everything went quiet. The rumour mill went into hyperdrive. He'd broken his neck. He was brain-damaged. He was dead. He'd never perform again. In truth, the injuries to his neck were not as serious as thought, but they did allow Bob to get off the treadmill. Having previously taken the cure, he was free of addiction and, due to the accident, also free of all contracts and obligations. After three or four years of relentless pressure, he was suddenly completely free. Dylan holed up in a big mansion in Woodstock, where, along with members of The Band, he kicked back and jammed in the basement of 'Big Pink', The Band's house, for pleasure. The tapes of those sessions became much sought-after bootlegs and later surfaced as *The Basement Tapes*.

Following this hiatus, Bob returned with an unexpected concert headlining in the Isle of Wight and an album with a country flavour. *John Wesley Harding* was a good album with some great songs but, with its country style and simpler songs, was a complete departure from the three colossi of his electric period. The thin wild mercury sound that he had developed had been superseded by something far less musically innovative.

The counterculture was bemused but was prepared to allow him an album or two to find his feet again. In his absence, the underground music scene that he had been pivotal in creating, whose sensitivities of equality, civil rights, anti-war and anti-establishment he had promulgated, had blossomed into a massive movement. The anti-war demonstrations and civil rights marches had taken on a new dimension. They had become mass movements fuelled by the underground bands and singers of the time. The establishment was rattled to its foundations. The 'revolution' was in search of a leader. There was hope and expectation that Dylan, who had been so instrumental in stirring the passions and initiating the rebellion, might step out of the shadows to assume a prominent role.

This was the very last thing that Bob wanted. He'd had more than enough of that first time around. He distanced himself from the whole hippie protest movement. They scared him. What we got now was a very unhip Dylan. No Cuban-heeled boots, tight trousers, polka-dot shirt and shades, no snarling invective, no multi-layered poetry, no challenging music. This Dylan looked and sounded very different. His appearance was ordinary. His sound was mellow. He even dueted with the ultraconservative Johnny Cash. While The Doors and Hendrix railed and raved, Bob crooned country tunes. This new incarnation was not strung out or cool. He'd moved on. This was a happy Dylan; a family man who no longer wanted to play that game. *Nashville Skyline* confirmed the change and by the time the *Self Portrait* album was released, nobody was in any doubt.

Dylan was not looking to be a leader again. He did not wish to fall back into that role. He no longer seemed to want to produce ground-breaking music but was content to go into semiretirement, to produce easy-listening music and kick back: 'Truth is I wanted to get out of the rat race'. Once again, his bemused disciples had been wrong-footed by a change of direction.

This new Dylan seemed to have moulted, to have shucked off the layers of protective 'cool' personas he had previously assumed. This new clean-cut, baby-faced version seemed completely uncool. No James Dean swagger, no authentic bohemian scruffiness. Even the poetry had evaporated. There were even questions as to whether this reinvented Dylan with his simpler music was not an imposter. A J Webberman started going through Dylan's trash bins to prove he was fake and set up the BDLF – the Bob Dylan Liberation Front.

Following the Isle of Wight, Bob seemed to fade away. It was George Harrison who coaxed him back into the forefront with an appearance at the Bangladesh concert and collaboration on a song on the *New Morning* album. By now, the sixties were coming to an end. The underground scene was imploding and the counterculture dissolving into a mess of hard drugs and violence. But for Dylan, *New Morning* pointed the way towards a new burst of creativity and a re-emergence. As with the sixties, the seventies were to hold many ups and downs and twists and turns for Bob. But that's another story.

Bob began the decade hustling to get noticed, eager for any exposure, a fiery ball of energy, trying desperately to develop a rebel persona, and ended it as a recluse, a family man, frantically trying to shed that rebel persona and live a quiet life out of the spotlight. In the beginning, his reputation was based on his complex poetic songs and themes of social conscience. By 1970, the poetry had all but evaporated and the content of nearly all his songs was much tamer, even banal.

Bob Dylan (1962)

Personnel:
Bob Dylan: acoustic guitar, vocals and harmonica
John Hammond: producer
Label: Colombia
Recorded at Colombia Studio A
Release date: March 1962
Highest chart position: UK: 13, USA: -

From the moment he arrived in Greenwich Village, Bob was a human dynamo, into everything, bursting with energy and manically throwing himself into the scene. He'd play anywhere, passing the basket round for small change, living hand to mouth, partying and jamming to all hours, crashing on couches and floors, talking incessantly, copying, pinching and exchanging chords, tales and songs. Greenwich Village was a melting pot. He was soaking it all up.

Bob was carefully cultivating his image as a rough-living, experienced roustabout in the Guthrie mould. He copied Guthrie's style, played a lot of his songs and even based his image on Woody's casual working clothes – an image that looked thrown together but was, in fact, agonised over. Part of the mystique he was studiously creating was the mythology of his earlier life, all carefully designed to put distance between his present incarnation and the ordinary middle-class upbringing he had experienced. Small-town middle class was not cool, not the image he wished to project. Bob Dylan was a construct, complete with an exciting, mythologised past.

There is some doubt as to when he completely left his former life behind. I had a friend (also called Bob) who was hitch-hiking around the States at the time and scrounging jobs wherever he could. In 1960, he ended up in Greenwich Village and managed to get a gig, because of his English accent, introducing acts in Gerdes Folk City. There was no pay, but Mike Porco supplied him with beer and food. That suited him fine. He remembered introducing Dylan onto the stage as Robert Zimmerman. Bob gave him a very dark look for his troubles. His recollection of Bob was of a very self-assured young man, with a brash, arrogant manner. He wasn't impressed with him or his music, finding the music too raw and abrasive and Bob's attitude rather aloof – my friend Bob was more a lover of traditional folk music – but he was taken with Bob's girlfriend (who would have been Suze Rotolo) and attempted to chat her up while Bob was playing (to no avail). Maybe the construction of his image was still a work in progress? Suze Rotolo claimed in her memoir not to have known him as Zimmerman, that only slipping out by accident when she stumbled across his draft card. Maybe my friend Bob's memory was playing tricks with him?

One of the consequences of Bob's lifestyle was that he soon began to play with a number of other people and was often found on stage supporting other acts, mainly playing harmonica, on which he was very proficient, or as a second guitar and supporting vocal. He was rapidly making a name for himself. These interactions led to other work and recording sessions. The first of these recording sessions was to play harmonica on Harry Belafonte's recording of 'Midnight Special'. Following that, he was used for a Caroline Hester recording session. This was incredibly fortuitous. Caroline recorded for Colombia Records and her producer was John Hammond. John was intrigued by this young man who was making such an impact in Greenwich Village and had fortuitously just received a favourable review in the New York Times that very week. Prior to the sessions, he visited Caroline's apartment to organise the arrangements, enticed Bob to sing a few songs for him and obviously recognised the talent. This led to Dylan signing for Columbia Records. For Bob, this was a major coup. Not only had Bob rapidly risen to prominence in such a cut-throat environment where most performers simply fell by the wayside, but he had secured a contract with a major label – not some small specialist label such as Vanguard, which many of the others had to be content with. Bob was as near as an overnight success. What was even stranger was that Bob's raw style was far from the flavour of the month. Folk music was a backwater. The most successful exponents were the more sophisticated folk groups such as the Greenbriar Boys or New City Ramblers or debonair folk singers like Joan Baez, queen of the folk movement. It was extremely hard to imagine Bob's unsophisticated style ever being commercial. John Hammond must have seen something and been incredibly persuasive with the board. Not only that but as a producer, he did not attempt to smooth Dylan out, polish up his performance or make it more commercial; he gave him his head, recorded what Dylan did without frills or a great deal of production and left it at that.

Incidentally, the third of Dylan's ventures into recording as a backing harmonica player was for a 1962 recording of the blues musicians Big Joe Williams and Victoria Spivey. These came out as the 1962 album *Three Kings and a Queen* (later outtakes came out as *Three Kings and a Queen Vol. 2*).

Bob also appeared under the pseudonym Blind Boy Grunt to avoid contractual obligations on a large number of Broadside recordings (three songs were officially released on the compilation album *Broadside Ballads Vol. 1*: 'John Brown', 'Only a Hobo', and 'Talking Devil'). He also later backed Happy Traum on a version of his own song 'Let Me Die in My Footsteps'. Using the same pseudonym, he also backed both Richard Farina and Eric Von Schmidt on their album projects.

When this 20-year-old Dylan had been asked in to sign the contract for Colombia, he was in a euphoric haze. He would have signed anything. He just looked at the writing at the top that said Columbia Records and signed, trusting John Hammond not to screw him over. At that signing, John gave Dylan a couple of unreleased acetates to listen to, recordings of artists that he thought Bob might relate to – The Dellmore Brothers, country singers, and an album by the blues singer Robert Johnson. John informed Dylan that Robert Johnson could 'whip anybody'. When Bob put it on his record player, he was instantly blown away. He couldn't believe the level of musicianship, the structure of the songs and poetic imagery. In a euphoric state, he rushed around to Dave Van Ronk's to play him this astounding masterpiece. Dave was less enthusiastic, calling it derivative, but that did not deter Bob. He spent ages playing and playing the album, picking the songs and lyrics to pieces to see how Johnson had put them together. It was an epiphany.

At around the same time, Suze had taken him to a Berthold Brecht play where he had been completely bowled over by the song 'Pirate Jenny'. Another song that Bob would dissect and marvel at. The building blocks of songwriting were being assembled.

That first album was not greatly carved out of Bob's stage act. Indeed, it left out most of the regular songs Dylan was performing at the time. He seemed reticent to reveal too much. Instead, in preparation for the recording sessions, he set about feverishly scanning friend's record collections for tracks to perform – many of which seemed to have a big Jesus theme. Nonetheless, the album reflected the wide range of material that he had been exposed to and subsequently adopted. He was adept at learning songs. While crashing at peoples' apartments, he would avidly devour their record collections. Bob claimed to be able to learn a song after only hearing it once. Quite a feat. The result was an album of earthy folk-blues and folk with only a couple of Bob's originals.

The sessions were spartan, recorded quickly in three afternoons, with just Bob on his guitar and harmonica, nothing added. They came across with a lot of force. The only sign of Bob's inexperience in the studio (John Hammond said that he spat his P's and hissed his S's and often turned away from the mic but refused to play songs twice), and the nerves he must have been feeling, was the speed of delivery. A number of the songs could have benefitted from a slower pace.

Ironically, the two Dylan tracks 'Song to Woody', in which he paid homage to his hero, and 'Talkin' New York', based on a Guthrie number, were dominant, but none of the Woody Guthrie songs that had been so prevalent in his sets were recorded. Even at this early-stage Bob had already moved on. Though he was still visiting Woody in the sanitorium, still singing his songs on stage, still mimicking his image, it was as if his debut album was a farewell to Woody.

I was only thirteen at the time of the album's release, but I was already a music nut. At that age, I was besotted with Buddy Holly, Eddie Cochran, Little Richard and The Shadows as well as avidly listening to all the current pop that was being played on Radio Luxemburg. I was still a year or two away from being introduced to the blues and Woody Guthrie. The Beatles hadn't yet happened, but I had been introduced to Joan Baez by an older girl with beatnik pretensions, and I liked Joan. I was young and open to new music.

My friend Charlie Mutton first played me the album. I remember being sat down as he reverently placed the album on his Dansette and I was handed the cover to read. I studied the cover, depicting a cherubic Dylan looking so fresh-faced that he didn't look as if he'd started to shave. He certainly was different to anybody I knew, in his corduroy black cap and fur-lined brown jacket. We both had basic Dansette record players back then and records were special. The vinyl was handled with great care and the cover pawed over. Mutt played both sides while I listened intently and read the cover notes.

I can't say that I was too impressed. The album did not bowl me over. However, I was not put off by it and quite enjoyed some of the tracks. It was just too raw and earthy for my young ears. I do remember being bemused as Mutt earnestly explained that Dylan was the next big thing and if he released a single, it would undoubtedly be a top ten hit.

I remember thinking that was extremely unlikely. I found it impossible to imagine anything as unsophisticated as this getting in the charts. It just shows how prophetic Mutt was and how wrong I could be. There are currently 257 different reissues of this album!

Although the album didn't set the world on fire, only selling 5000 copies on release, it did serve to raise Bob's status locally and bring him to the attention of a wider audience.

'You're No Good' (Jessie Fuller)
My first taste of Dylan started with a neatly strummed acoustic guitar, as Bob sets out on a cover of this Jesse Fuller folk-blues number. Despite the mournful lyrics about a no-good two-timing girl who is mistreating him, Bob makes it sound quite cheerful and even adds in a chuckle. There is that underlying hint of the mischievous Chaplin delivery, although it doesn't spill over into comedy. Even the harmonica bridge is spritely and playful. The vocal delivery is at times, a bit nasal and, at other times, forced for emphasis as the number builds in intensity and speed as it progresses.

'Talkin' New York' (Bob Dylan)
The first of Bob's originals delivered in his best Woody Guthrie talking blues style, complete with the same strummed guitar pattern and harmonica. This song is a commentary on Bob's arrival, his impressions of hitch-hiking into New York, and tells the story of how he attempts to get himself established on the folk scene. It is a complete mimicry of Woody down to the voice, with its elevated vocal lift at the end of the verse and added observation. He has the intonation perfect, even the way Woody mispronounces words – as with 'green witch village'. There is an oblique reference to Woody as 'a very great man', using some of Guthrie's lines about joining the union and paying his dues, then making reference to 'rob you with a fountain pen' from 'Pretty Boy Floyd'.

16

The wry and social observation is tinged with the same sarcastic humour that Woody deployed. As a mimic, Bob was already a master.

'In My Time of Dying' (Blind Willie Johnson – arranged by Bob Dylan)
There's a change of style for the third track. We're into a harder style of guitar playing with plucked strings and even flourishes of slide guitar (using Suze's metallic lipstick holder) on what is a classic blues song. The song was first recorded by Blind Willie Johnson but had its roots in earlier unrecorded blues renditions. Bob based his performance more on the Josh White version and may have heard Josh play it at the Gaslight Club.

Bob delivers the song in an intense anguished manner with a voice strained with emotion. For a 20-year-old to be dealing with death in this way is difficult, but Bob pulls it off with a masterful performance of both guitar and vocal.

'Man of Constant Sorrow' (Traditional – arranged by Bob Dylan)
After the intensity of Bob's blues interpretation, we're taken off to the mountains of Kentucky for a trip into the world of Dick Burnett, a blind fiddle player, who recorded the song in 1913. What is already clear is that Bob is looking for variety. He has selected this hillbilly track as a contrast to the blues.

I would suggest that Bob chose this track with the idea of reinforcing his image as being a hard-travelling rambling man who rode the blinds along with the hobos – an image that was rather at odds with his real background. He delivers the song with a haunting, wistful delivery, voice wavering above a strummed and plucked guitar and melancholy harmonica.

'Fixin' to Die' (Bukka White)
Although this is based on the Bukka White song (delivered by Bukka with typical delta bottleneck guitar) it has differences in both melody and words. We're back into another forceful blues song. Dylan produces a gutsy performance, the vocal forceful and clear, the guitar powerfully strummed with emphasising picked notes between verses.

'Pretty Peggy-O' (Traditional – arranged by Bob Dylan)
Bob takes this traditional Scottish folk song on a different journey. His guitar strumming is overlaid with harmonica as he sets off on a different tack, attacking the verses with panache and even a whoop or two, hitting the heavier bass strings behind the vocals to give it weight and punch with lighter flurries between verses.

The song is hundreds of years old and has been through many mutations, such as 'The Bonnie Lass of Fyvie'. The original tells of a Scots maid rejecting the advances of an English officer. Translocated to America, it took on civil war overtones. Bob gives it an exuberant outing.

'Highway 51' (Curtis Jones)

Dylan raises the tempo further with a series of fierce strumming patterns, striking the bass strings for added impact on this Curtis Jones cover. Curtis was a blues pianist who wrote this song about Highway 51 which stretched from New Orleans to Canada. A route that was used by many blues singers and is rich in history.

On this track, as on others on this debut album, Bob's voice rises into strained, anguished tones as he pours everything into the performance. Interesting to note that the guitar strumming has similarities to that on 'It's Alright Ma, I'm Only Bleeding'.

'Gospel Plow' (Traditional – arranged by Bob Dylan)

Bob turns this old spiritual (also known as 'Hold On' or 'Keep Your Hands on the Plow'), based on a line from Luke's gospel, into an up-tempo race, setting the rhythm with an innovative fast harmonica pattern over a steady guitar strum that sets up a driving pace. Bob's rapid rasping vocals add to the blistering delivery to create a passionate version.

'Baby Let Me Follow You Down' (Traditional – arranged by Eric Von Schmidt)

Bob slows the pace down and delivers a mellow vocal on this old blues number first recorded in 1935 by the State Street Boys (featuring Big Bill Broonzy and Jazz Gillum). There is a spoken intro over the top of a restrained guitar riff in which Dylan explains how he learnt the song from Eric Von Schmidt, a regular performer in Greenwich Village, who he met in Harvard. The song was originally called 'Don't Tear My Clothes' and has a simple repeating chorus and not too many words.

The Animals went on to produce an electric blues version, with more verses, on their first album.

'House of the Rising Sun' (Traditional – arranged by Dave Van Ronk)

The song has its roots in English sixteenth-century folk music and has proceeded through myriad versions with both male and female perspectives. It tells a cautionary tale of either prostitution or drinking and gambling at the bawdy house called The Rising Sun.

The song has been sung and adapted by countless people. Woody Guthrie did a version, but it was Dave Van Ronk's arrangement that Dylan copied. Dave was due to record the song on his next album when Dylan stole his thunder. This resulted in a big bust-up with Dave and strained relationships for a long time.

Bob's voice is deeply nuanced as he delivers the story in a controlled, insistent manner over delicately strummed strings. The song slowly builds as Bob's voice soars and wails, the last verse wrung out in agonised passion through a tortured larynx.

The Animals produced a storming electric version of the song that became a mega-hit. That and Burdon's version of 'Baby Let Me Follow You Down' were all part of the impetus for Bob to later go electric.

'Freight Train Blues' (John Lair – arranged by Mississippi Fred McDowell)

Once again a change of mood as Bob launches into a hillbilly country song written in the 1930s for Red Foley. Bob is clearly enjoying himself as he sets off at breakneck speed with some intricate nifty harmonica and guitar setting the pace of a fast-moving locomotive. The speed is so fast that he has trouble fitting all the words into the space. The ends of the word 'blues' is elongated out into an 'ooooooooo' that mimics a train whistle. On the second verse, it is so long a note that Bob gives a slight chuckle, pleased with himself. This fun track makes quite a contrast to the emotional one that precedes it.

'Song to Woody' (Bob Dylan)

'Song to Woody' is the second original track on the album and another homage to his great mentor. The melody is based on Guthrie's '1913 Massacre' and delivered in the classic Woody style in both its guitar and vocal delivery and composition.

Bob portrays himself as a rambling man following in Woody's footsteps. He talks of the new world that 'Looks like it's dyin', but it's hardly been born' and eulogises Woody 'Not many men have done what you've done'.

In the last verse, he lists Woody's fellow travellers and parodies his words, 'Come with the dust and gone with the wind'. He ends by saying, 'The very last thing that I'd want to do is to say I've been hittin' some hard travellin' too'. Woody must have been touched when the nineteen-year-old Dylan sang it to him in the Greystone Park State Hospital in New Jersey, where he spent the last five years of his life.

'See That My Grave is Kept Clean' (Blind Lemon Jefferson)

The album ends with a return to the intensity of the earlier blues tracks. This time he applies it to a Blind Lemon Jefferson track recorded first in 1927 and covered by many other blues artists, including Lightnin' Hopkins and Texas Alexander. However, none of those blues guys manage to capture this level of distress. Bob is forcing the air through vocal cords that sound as though they are being crushed in a vice. The picked strumming with bass string runs, punctuated with an occasional thud, provide a base for Bob to plead over as he anticipates his last days. He may not have the smoothest of voices, a trifle nasal and limited, but what it may lack in quality, it certainly makes up in intensity.

It has been an experience. Bob has taken us on an odyssey through death, unrequited love, vagrancy, prostitution, drunkenness and religion, with a smattering of homage to a hero and fun thrown in. Perhaps not the recipe for commercial success?

Outtakes

There were four outtakes from the session and one other track that was briefly released as a single.

'House Carpenter' (Traditional)

A song that was a Dylanised version of the sixteenth-century Scottish ballad 'The Daemon Lover' that, for reasons unknown, was not included on that debut album but would eventually be released on the *Bootleg Series Vol. 1*.

The omission could not have been because of the performance, which was nigh on perfect. The fast strumming with picking showcased Bob's guitar skills at their best. It fairly rollicks along. The tale is delivered in Bob's most articulate and smooth delivery. He begins with a spoken intro over strummed guitar: 'Here's a story of a ghost come back from out of the sea, come to take his bride away from the house carpenter'. It has the feel of the kind of storytelling that would later emerge in Bob's own songwriting as with 'The Ballad of Hollis Brown'. I'm sure it would have only added to the range and variety of the album which showcased the many genres of music that Bob was inspired by and was busy absorbing.

It is another example of the way Bob had chosen songs for the album. For the most part, they were songs that did not appear in his live repertoire. He had assembled them from many sources and selected tracks. Although the song was played in folk circles, it was not part of Dylan's set.

'He Was a Friend of Mine' (Traditional)

The song was eventually released on *The Bootleg Series Vol. 1*.

'He Was a Friend of Mine' was a song first recorded by Leadbelly in 1935 and then Smith Casey in 1939 entitled 'Shorty George'. Bob probably picked it up from Rolf Cahn's 1961 album with Eric Von Schmidt; it was Rolf who changed the name to 'He Was a Friend of Mine', though Bob told Robert Shelton that he heard it from Blind Arvella Gray.

Bob is in whimsical mood as he plays this melancholy song. The guitar is picked and strummed as the harmonica plays the melody. The sad tale is one of the lonely death of an itinerant hobo who dies on the road. Bob sings it beautifully in mellow, respectful mood, a song that eulogises the type of lifestyle that Bob is trying to own. It fits the new image. Probably considered too sweet and restrained for inclusion on the album.

'Man On The Street' (Traditional/Bob Dylan)

Released on *The Bootleg Series Vol. 1*.

Bob adapted this from a traditional song sung by Pete Seeger, 'The Young Man Who Wouldn't Hoe Corn'. It is based around two chords and continues

Bob's wish to identify with the down and outs, lamenting a hobo who was found dead on the streets and the off-hand manner in which his death was dealt with. It was another performance that was probably too restrained to include on the first album. A shame. The later Gaslight performance was much more dynamic.

'Ramblin' Blues' (Woody Guthrie)
Woody Guthrie had been the backbone of Dylan's prerecording era. Not only had he adopted his style, intonation and look, but he had introduced a number of Woody's songs into his stage act and even more in informal gatherings. However, this was the only Guthrie song to feature in the sessions. I think Dylan knew that it was already time to move on and his 'Song to Woody' was his parting gift. It is also telling that it is the only outtake that remains unreleased.

'Connecticut Cowboy'
A spoken-word intro for the song 'You're No Good' that was recorded at a different time and never used because it could not be easily grafted onto the track with the current technology.

Hoodoo Reissue Bonus Tracks (2013)
The Hoodoo label reissue of Bob's debut album contained a number of unreleased tracks. Mainly radio or other live performances from 1961 and 1962 with a couple of interesting rarities.

'Mixed Up Confusion (Single version)' (Bob Dylan)
Reviewed later.

'Roll On John (Live)' (Traditional – arranged by Bob Dylan) (WBAI Radio, New York 1962)
'Hard Times in New York (Live)' (Bob Dylan) (WBAI Radio, New York 1962)
'Smokestack Lightning (Live)' (Chester Burnett) (WBAI Radio, New York 1962)
'Stealin' Stealin' (Live)' (Gus Gannon) (WBAI Radio, New York 1962)
'Baby Please Don't Go (Live)' (Big Joe Williams) (WBAI Radio, New York 1962)
'The Death of Emmett Till (Live)' (Bob Dylan) (WBAI Radio, New York 1962)
'Man on the Street (Live)' (Bob Dylan) (Carnegie Chapter Hall, New York 1961)
'Omie Wise (Live)' (Traditional) (Riverside Church for WRVR Radio, New York 1961)

'Don't Think Twice it's Alright (Live)' (Bob Dylan) (Gaslight Café, New York 1961)
'The Girl I Left Behind (Live)' (Traditional – arranged by Bob Dylan) (Oscar Brand's Folk Song Festival, New York 1961)
'Blowing in the Wind (Live)' (Bob Dylan) (Broadside Show, WBAI Radio, New York 1962)

'House of the Rising Sun' (Traditional)
A version of the song, that the producer Tom Wilson heavily overdubbed with electric instruments, was included on the *Highway 61 Interactive* CD-Rom.

The Freewheelin' Bob Dylan (1963)

Personnel:
Bob Dylan: acoustic guitar, piano, vocals and harmonica
Dick Wellstood: piano
Howie Collins: guitar
Bruce Langhorne: guitar
Leonard Gaskin: bass
Herb Lovelle: drums
Art Davis: bass
George Barnes: guitar
John Hammond, Tom Wilson: producer
Gene Ramey: bass
Label: Colombia
Recorded at Colombia Studio A
Release date: May 1963
Highest chart positions: UK: 1 US: 22

This second album was originally titled *Bob Dylan's Blues*. An album that nearly didn't happen. Following the poor showing of the debut album, Colombia wanted to dump him, but John Hammond argued forcibly to give him one more chance. How lucky were we?

What a difference a year makes. Bob was enthused with a new confidence. He had become a major player on the Greenwich Village circuit and was in demand with a number of radio performances. Although the first album had not sold many copies, it had served to enhance his reputation. Bob was taking off.

The major change was that he was coming out of the shadow of Woody Guthrie and the old blues and folk singers and emerging as a major songwriter. This was the time when many of his greatest numbers were written and recorded. His songwriting was progressing at such a rate that the recording sessions could not keep up, the songs recorded at the early sessions being shelved as they were superseded by superior originals.

In 1962, following the release of his first album, Bob signed a publishing deal with the Leeds subsidiary Duchess Music. They suggested producing a songbook which proved a big impetus and set Bob off madly writing songs. He rapidly produced seven demos for them. When Albert Grossman took over, he wanted to sign Bob up to Witmark and Son (a subsidiary of Music Publishers' Holding Company) because he had an arrangement where he would get half the profit. Bob bought his contract back from Leeds and signed. Over the next few years, he made many demos for Witmark (much bootlegged), all of which, including the Leeds ones, came out many years later on *The Bootleg Series Vol. 7*.

This was the time when he began writing topical songs of a social and political nature that the media began to call 'protest songs'. At the time, he'd fallen in love and set up an apartment on West 4th Street with Suze Rotolo. Suze's family were very left-wing communists and the relationship, along with access to a wealth of books, poems and records that her family owned, fired Bob up. Unfortunately, Suze's family did not take to Bob and tried their hardest to split them up. This culminated in Suze's mother convincing Suze to take time out to go to Italy to study art. This separation caused great heartache. Bob poured his soul out in letters and songs. His emotions and frustrations were laid bare. The fruits of this relationship were to be found in a legacy of brilliant anti-war, civil rights love songs. The quality of these songs began impacting the media. The poetic content was being recognised. Bob had begun to be taken seriously. For once, 'Pop' music was being considered as a serious art form. On a negative note, it also caused the media to start calling him 'the spokesman of a generation', a term that Bob detested and which was to have a big impact on him and what he did.

The second huge bearing on his career was Albert Grossman. Albert recognised Bob's potential and jumped in to manage him. This propelled Bob into a much greater professional orbit. Albert began to demand higher billing and more money, negotiating in an aggressive manner. He was a big brusque man with whom it was hard to argue. He also put together and managed the folk trio Peter, Paul and Mary and had them turn Bob's 'Blowing in the Wind' into a chart-friendly single and a top ten hit. It rapidly became a major anthem of the sixties. Albert took exception to the redneck John Hammond and fought to have him replaced as producer with the Afro-American Jazz producer Tom Wilson who he believed would be more sympathetic to Bob's material and ideas.

The third factor was Joan Baez. She was the undisputed Queen of the Folk Scene. Her act and albums were basically all traditional folk songs, but she was quick to recognise Bob's talent and the quality of his songwriting. She began to record his songs and took this ragamuffin songwriter on tour with her, introducing him to a wider audience. Soon they were going to be referred to as the King and Queen of folk.

In January 1963, Bob was invited to perform in a BBC TV drama called *Madhouse on Castle Street*. He took advantage of the free flight to go early to England in December 1962 and immersed himself in the London folk scene. In particular, the young Martin Carthy and Bob Davenport related to him and taught in many of the traditional English folk songs, the melodies (and sometimes words) of which he was to make use of in his own songwriting. As well as performing in the drama, he recorded four songs for use in it: 'Blowing in the Wind', 'Hang Me, O Hang Me', 'Cuckoo Bird', and 'Ballad of the Gliding Swan'.

By the time Bob went into the studio to record his second album, he was beginning to soar. There were eight sessions for the album, three of which were electric. This was quite revolutionary and demonstrated a major trend in

Bob's thinking. He'd started off as a rocker idolising Little Richard and strayed into the world of folk. Now he was already looking to combine the two.

Bob's songwriting was on fire. He had gone into the studio with a mound of newly written self-penned songs. Altogether they recorded 36 songs; only thirteen were used on the album and one as a single. It meant that there were a lot of outtakes.

Charlie and I played the album and were impressed with Bob's songs. By this time, I had been introduced to authentic blues by my mate Dick Brunning, so I was more accustomed to the rawer sounds, but even so, I found my tender young ears preferring the more sanitised versions. Bob's nasally drawl was still a little too rough.

Unbeknown to both of us, that second album was imbued with controversy. Bob was already writing a lot of his own material, songs which deployed a lot of wit and social content (such as 'Bear Mountain Massacre'). The one that stood out was the humorous and cutting 'John Birch Society Blues'.

The attention Bob was receiving under the promotion of his agent Albert Grossman secured him a much-coveted slot on the hugely prestigious Ed Sullivan Show. This was intended to gain maximum publicity ahead of the album release. There was much expectation. At the rehearsal, it all went wrong. Bob was intending to showcase 'John Birch Society Blues' in the three numbers he had been allotted. Following the rehearsal, representatives of Ed Sullivan approached the Dylan camp and asked them to replace the John Birch number with something else. It was considered too controversial and likely to result in a strident reaction from the extreme right-wing group. Bob went apoplectic and stormed off, refusing to appear on the show. This had massive repercussions for Colombia, not only depriving them of a great slot in which they had hoped to promote their new acquisition but also alerting them to the controversial nature of the song. The album had already been pressed up and circulated. High drama. Albert Grossman, always looking for the positive angle – all publicity is good publicity – managed to smooth things out. He negotiated a compromise. A rethink of the album was carried out. Bob was furious at the censorship but powerless to do anything about it.

In all, four tracks were taken off the album, ('John Birch Paranoid Blues', 'Let Me Die in My Footsteps', 'Rambling, Gambling Willie' and 'Rocks and Gravel'). They were replaced with four of Bob's newer recordings: 'Girl from the North Country', 'Masters of War', 'Talkin' World War III Blues', and 'Bob Dylan's Dream'. People were made aware. The album still contained a few of Bob's toughest songs. Bob's credibility was not dented. He was placated. The original pressing was withdrawn, destroyed and the revised pressing released. Dylan had his second album and Colombia was still on board. Colombia thought they'd dealt with it, but a few copies of the original pressing of the LP with the four deleted tracks have turned up over the years, despite Columbia's attempts to destroy them all. Those albums fetch enormous prices when they come up for sale.

The cover of the album reflected the Dylan of those days. Although it was carefully staged, the photographer, Don Hunstein, after taking numerous shots in Dylan's apartment on West 4th Street in Greenwich Village, asked them to walk up and down the icy February street, hoping to catch a more informal shot. The picture he came up with captured it all. Here was a fresh-faced young 21-year-old Bob with his young girlfriend Suze Rotolo hanging on his arm, cuddling into him. Dylan was wearing a thin brown jacket, blue jeans and boots. Hunched against the cold, hands deep in pockets, ambling down the middle of the street, Bob appears to be saying something and Suze is grinning. Image was everything. Not only did it capture that youthful love and vitality but also the rebelliousness. Dylan liked it because he thought it made him look like James Dean.

This is the period when Bob started writing long epic poetry such as 'Last Thoughts on Woody Guthrie' which he read aloud at the New York Town Hall concert in 1963. He adorned the back of both *The Times They Are A-Changin* and *Another Side of Bob Dylan* with these fascinating poetic prose compositions. He also wrote a similar poem for the Joan Baez album *Joan Baez in Concert, Part 2* and the Peter, Paul And Mary album *In the Wind*. Peter Paul And Mary were in the Albert Grossman camp and it had been Paul who had first alerted Albert to Bob's potential.

Three months after the release of *Freewheelin'*, Bob, along with Joan Baez and other singers, was invited to perform at the civil rights march in Washington where Martin Luther King gave his famous 'I Have A Dream' speech. Bob sang four songs – 'Only a Pawn in Their Game', 'When the Ship Comes In', 'Blowin' in the Wind,' and 'Keep Your Eyes on the Prize'.

'Blowin' in the Wind' (Bob Dylan)

Bob claims to have written this anti-war anthem in The Commons coffee house opposite The Gaslight, a favourite haunt of folk musicians, in just ten minutes flat. The melody was based on the spiritual 'No Auction Block'.

The song was the first of Bob's topical 'protest' songs to be recorded and made an immediate impact on his audience, with its strong anti-war and civil rights themes, when played live. Its simplicity belied the straightforward strength of its message. Unlike previous topical songs with specific issues about Donald White or Emmitt Till, the target of this song was more general:

> I still say that some of the biggest criminals are those that turn their heads away when they see wrong and know it's wrong. I'm only 21 years old and I know that there's been too many wars ... You people over 21, you're older and smarter.

The idea for the song might well have been sparked by Woody Guthrie's comment about newspapers blowing around in the streets of New York. The idea for the song being ambiguous – either the answers were there to be found or they weren't, tapping right into the zeitgeist of the time.

Although the Chad Mitchell Trio recorded the number first, their rendition was delayed and Albert Grossman had the song recorded by his manufactured group Peter, Paul and Mary, who had an enormous hit with it and propelled Dylan into the stratosphere in the process.

Bob's version is acoustic with simple strumming and harmonica playing, his voice clear and full of passion as he articulates the lyrics clearly. The repeating structure of the poem reinforces the message.

'Girl From the North Country' (Traditional – arrangement Bob Dylan and Martin Carthy)

Bob learnt the basis of this song, both lyrically and musically, from Martin Carthy on his trip to England in December 1962. Martin taught him his arrangement of the traditional English song 'Scarborough Fayre'. At the time, Bob's relationship with Suze Rotolo was having trouble and they were patching things up. The song could have been directed at her or his ex-girlfriend Echo or even Bonnie Beecher – perhaps all three – or it's just a song he learnt while over in England.

The delivery features a delightfully soft, delicate, yet bright-picked guitar. Bob's voice, with a slight nasal edge, is full of longing, his diction clear, carrying the melody well with some wistful harmonica towards the end.

'Masters of War' (Bob Dylan)

'Masters of War' is the ultimate anti-war song – still unsurpassed in its venom to this day. Bob rains his fury down on the politicians, weapons manufacturers and dealers, and the military who cause so much death and destruction. Never has a song before wished death upon these evil purveyors of slaughter. At the time, the cold war between the West and Russia was clouding everybody's life. The spectre of war hung in the air that everyone breathed. Broadside magazine printed the words and music accompanied by a drawing that Suze Rotolo had done to go with them of someone carving up the world with a knife and fork while a poor family looks on – incredibly powerful. A song packed with chilling, goose-bump-inducing poetic lines as Bob's stark accusatory warning is snarled over a bed of repeating acoustic strums. He spits the words with vitriol: 'A world war can be won, you want me to believe. But I see through your eyes and I see through your brain like I see through the water that runs down my drain.' The lyrics are universal and relevant to all wars. In it, Bob tells the warmongers that 'You ain't worth the blood that runs through your veins.'

The melody for the song comes from the English folk song 'Nottamun Town' with the arrangement by folksinger Jean Ritchie. Bob was going through a phase of adapting the lyrics of traditional folk songs he had learnt from Martin Carthy and Bob Davenport.

'Down the Highway' (Bob Dylan)

Suze had been packed off to study art by her mother in an attempt to split them up. Dylan was bereft and poured out his woe in an attempt at catharsis in this twelve-bar blues. He was lonely, he missed her and it hurt.

The guitar pattern is fabulous. It builds and reconciles as Bob pours out a story depicting himself as a lonely, lost itinerant gambling man, fueling the image he had constructed for himself, eager to meet up with his lost love (Suze) in the middle of the ocean.

'Bob Dylan's Blues' (Bob Dylan)

Bob hides his misery at the absence of Suze behind a mask of lightheartedness. It seems that the Lone Ranger and Tonto are not going to come to his rescue any time soon. He's lost, wandering around New York. He doesn't want any women or fun; he just wants his woman back. He's down. All he can imagine is to go and rob a bank.

The song structure is upbeat, with a spoken intro over the acoustic guitar with bursts of harmonica. He's trying to jolly himself out of his mood.

'A Hard Rain's a-Gonna Fall' (Bob Dylan)

One of Bob's early masterpieces. A lyrically complicated poem/song constructed around the question-and-answer pattern of the traditional English ballad entitled 'Lord Randall'. Dylan claimed to have written the song in response to the Cuban missile crisis. He said that each line was actually a poem that he did not think he was going to have time to write because we were all going to be destroyed in a nuclear holocaust. This was a piece of opportunism. In actual fact, he had written the song a good month earlier while hanging out with Wavy Gravy and Tom Paxton in their shared apartment.

Written on the typewriter using the symbolism of Rimbaud's poetry, Bob was pulling out all manner of human crisis – war, environmental issues, racism, civil rights, social injustice, violence and extremism – that he had gleaned from reading through endless news microfilm in the library. The poem highlighted all the catastrophic mistakes humanity was guilty of – a litany of disaster. When the Cuban missile crisis occurred, Bob saw the opportunity to marry it to the crisis.

The poetic symbolism is deep and often ambiguous. What is sometimes apparent is later found to be wrong. Bob himself often either clarifies or further muddies the waters:

No, it's not atomic rain; it's just a hard rain. It isn't the fallout rain. I mean some sort of end that's just gotta happen... In the last verse, when I say, "the pellets of poison are flooding the waters," that means all the lies that people get told on their radios and in their newspapers.

It is certainly poetry that rattles in your brain, sometimes with clarity, often opaque, but always teasing your sensibilities, forcing you to think and wonder.

When Allen Ginsberg, the Beat poet, first heard this song, he realised that Bob was the next generation of poets. The torch was being passed on.

The guitar is in a drop D tuning with a capo on the third fret. Dylan sings in a Guthrie-esque voice that almost recites the poem over a bed of strummed guitar. The repetitive nature of both the lines of poetry and musical structure reinforces the strength of the lyric. It engages the mind in a reverie of analysis and flashes of understanding. Seven minutes soon pass on a voyage of interpretation as it sucks you into its mesmeric depths. No matter how many times you hear it there is always something new to discover or wonder at. Despite its musical simplicity and repetitive nature, it never fails to engage.

'Bob Dylan's Dream' (Traditional/Bob Dylan)
Once again, the melody for this song was taught by Martin Carthy over in England. Bob took the nineteenth-century English ballad 'Lady Franklin's Lament' – a song written to commemorate the tragic death of Lord Franklin in 1847 – and put new words to it.

What came out was a mournful burst of nostalgia; in the absence of Suze, Bob is basking in his misery and wishing everything could be back to how it had once been. In the context of a dream, he reflects back on the carefree days hanging out with his friends: 'I wish, I wish, I wish in vain, that we could sit simply in that room again.'

'Oxford Town' (Bob Dylan)
A civil rights song relating to the riots sparked off when the black student James Meredith tried to enrol at the University of Mississippi in Oxford. The incident inspired a number of prominent folk singers to declare their outrage at the way it was handled and the incipient racism so evident in Mississippi. Bob chose a lighter touch. While he catalogues the harsh treatment metered out by the police, leading to the deaths of two men and the horrendous prejudice, he sings it to a jaunty-sounding guitar and even manages to instil a touch of humour into the song, which serves to make the impact even greater.

'Talking World War III Blues' (Bob Dylan)
'Talking World War III Blues' takes us right back to the Woody Guthrie talking blues style. As in the past, it enabled him to address a serious issue by deploying humour. This was in the depths of the cold war, with the Cuban missile crisis causing a great deal of fear. The nuclear shelter industry was having a field day.

Bob was relating an imaginary dream in which he was the lone survivor of a nuclear war. Like all dreams, it has an inbuilt absurdity starting with him being down in the sewer system with his girlfriend when it all goes off, though she doesn't feature from that moment on. It then proceeds to relate various increasingly absurd situations, allowing Bob to find amusing scenarios in which he can ridicule various aspects of American society and lampoon conservatives.

The third world war in Bob's hands proves fertile ground for social observation and fun. The song featured strongly in Dylan's live act. At this point in time, he was still using his theatrical Chaplin-esque comedy.

'Corrina, Corrina' (Mississippi Sheiks/Bo Carter)

The acoustic version was used on the album with strummed and picked guitar. Bob uses a walking bass line while simultaneously plucking high notes. The voice is intense, but Bob expresses the beauty of the melody well. A haunting love song about a girl who has left him, choked with remorse. Another one to chalk up to Suze.

'Honey, Just Allow Me One More Chance' (Henry Thomas – arranged by Bob Dylan)

Henry 'Ragtime Texas' Thomas was a blues singer who recorded this song in 1927 under the title 'Honey, Won't You Allow Me One More Chance?'. Bob kept the same tempo and adapted the words.

Once again, Bob is airing his hurt and frustration at Suze's long absence. It was as if he was using his songs to send messages to her. When she finally returned from her long stay in Italy, their friends cajoled her for leaving Bob. They told her he had been moping around and expressing his pain to anyone who'd listen. Mind you, even after he'd got her back, it did not stop him from starting up an affair with Joan Baez, an affair that would split them up for good. While it is cloaked in humour, there is still an air of desperation.

Like all the other songs on the album, this was just Bob, his acoustic guitar and his harmonica which was wedged into his infamous metal holder that he positioned around his neck. It is based around A7 and G7 chords and includes Bob's characteristic harmonica refrains between each verse.

'I Shall Be Free' (Leadbelly – arranged by Bob Dylan)

The album ends with an adaptation of a Leadbelly song from the 1940s. Huddie had recorded it with Sonny Terry, Cisco Houston and Woody Guthrie. The title was 'We Shall Be Free' and was itself an adaptation of an old spiritual.

The frivolity of the track contrasts with the seriousness of the heavyweight offerings on the album. Yet even on these lighter efforts, Bob manages to put in some meaningful social comment.

Single
'Mixed Up Confusion' (Bob Dylan)
Personnel:
Bob Dylan: guitar: vocals

Bruce Langhorne: guitar
George Barnes: guitar
Dick Wellstood: piano
Gene Ramey: bass
Herb Lovelle: drums

This track was not included on the album but was briefly released as a single before being withdrawn. A strange choice as a single, being completely at odds with anything else on the album – recorded with a full band. Despite its fast tempo, it is not so much rock 'n' roll as country. The decision to experiment with a band was John Hammond's but I'm sure, given his early love of rock music, that Bob was not hard to persuade.

The choice of material for this experiment was perhaps a mistake. 'Mixed Up Confusion' was a throwaway track that Bob had written on a cab ride into the studio. Following the spoken intro, the song takes off at a pace verging on rockabilly. The harmonica, drums and piano are very much to the fore. They don't quite gel but they do create a discernible Dylan sound that he will return to in later electric recordings.

The lyrics reveal a Dylan who was already beginning to feel the pressure of being caught up in the music businesses spin drier: 'Too many people and they're all too hard to please.' 'Looking for some answers and I don't know who to ask'.

The single was put out but did not register anywhere and was quickly withdrawn.

'Corrina Corrina (Single version)' (Mississippi Sheiks/Bo Carter)
This version has the band backing with a light touch that is not intrusive. The drums and bass are subdued and sympathetic. Bob's voice is mellow, soft and croony; much more controlled. The end result is a softer, more melodic version to that of the acoustic album take.

'Blowin' in the Wind' b/w **'Don't Think Twice it's Alright'**
Both tracks are taken straight off the album.

Outtakes
'Talkin' John Birch Paranoid Blues' (Bob Dylan) (Freewheelin' Outtakes 2018)
This was the absolute heavyweight of all the outtakes – a song that formed a major part of his live performances and set the tone for what he stood for at that time. Just as Woody had done in the past, deploying this same talking blues, Bob used the form to take a controversial topical issue, charge it with humour and use it as a barbed weapon. The targets of his wit and venom were the anti-communist McCarthy purges and the extreme right-wing ultranationalist John Birch Society. He created an imbecilic paranoid character

who joined the John Birch Society and set about hunting commies all over the place. Not only hilarious but cutting.

In the song, he mentions George Lincoln Rockwell, the founder of the American Nazi Party who, dressed in Nazi uniform, picketed the movie *Exodus* (a film about the founding of Israel). *Exodus* was scripted by Dalton Trumbo, one of the writers obscenely blacklisted by McCarthy. This blacklisting of writers, performers and singers was highly inflammatory among the radical left-wing folkies. People like Pete Seeger had their careers ruined and were unable to work. In the land of the free, it did not do to cross McCarthy. Free speech did not really mean free speech.

Bob was to discover that when he attempted to include the song on his album and sing it on the prestigious Ed Sullivan show. The Ed Sullivan show was incredibly important and provided a springboard to a wider audience. When Bob was told at rehearsals to replace the track he stormed out of the show. Columbia Records then removed the track from the album. Both Ed Sullivan and Colombia Records were scared to bring the wrath of the powerful Birchers and McCarthyites down upon them. They played safe. As mentioned earlier, four tracks were removed from the early test pressing and hurriedly replaced with newer Bob Dylan songs. Though Bob was incensed with the censorship, he did not have enough clout to do anything about it.

'Baby, I'm in the Mood For You' (Bob Dylan) (released on Biograph & Freewheelin' Outtakes 2018)
A lightweight, repetitive piece of fun. A jolly song of little significance even though Bob tries hard to insert some life into it by using inflexions in his voice and adding a whoop or two. The lyric doesn't have too much going for it and the simplistic repeating verses do not allow for any depth or development.

'Baby Please Don't Go' (Big Joe Williams) (released on iTunes outtakes from No Direction Home & Freewheelin' Outtakes)
It was rare for Bob to do covers of other peoples' songs at this period of time as he was churning out so many of his own as can be seen from this huge catalogue of outtakes for the album. Big Joe Williams was a blues singer that Bob had seen playing in Greenwich Village. He'd been impressed with his power and stature as a hard-living blues guy. Joe had recorded this number in 1935, but it had its roots much further back than that with a number of variants, including 'Alabamy Bound' and 'Long John'. The song was made into a big hit in 1964 by Them, featuring Van Morrison.

Dylan does not try to do a straight cover of the track but instead injects his own arrangement. The result is incredibly powerful. Bob's voice is full of anger as he forces air across his tonsils, his guitar chords slashing and menacing. What really makes the track is the dominant bass. The persistent dark bubbling bass is so strong that it adds a great strength to what is a bravura performance.

This is such a brilliant effort that I can only suggest that it was left off the album because it was out of keeping with the acoustic material that made up the album. The other factor being that it wasn't a Dylan composition.

'Corrina, Corrina' (Mississippi Sheiks) (two alternative takes on Freewheelin' Outtakes 2018)
This was yet another variation of the track. Bob really liked the song and wanted to get a definitive take.

'Ballad of Hollis Brown' (Bob Dylan) (The Freewheelin' Outtakes. Re-recorded for Dylan's next album, The Times They Are A-Changin')
'Hollis Brown' was recorded for *The Times They Are A-Changin'* album. This early version is a little lighter, sung over a steady strummed guitar with no picking and has some great harmonica interludes.

The chord and verse structure are taken from the old English song, popular in the Appalachians, 'Pretty Polly'. The publishing contract with Leeds and then Witmark had spurred Bob onto a burst of creativity. At this time, Bob was mining a rich vein of songwriting by harnessing new lyrics to traditional melodies or adapting old songs. His output was enormous.

'The Death of Emmett Till' (Bob Dylan) (Freewheelin' Outtakes 2018)
This powerful track was never properly recorded for release on an album which is a great shame as I think it was one of Dylan's strongest. The song was written in Dylan's reporting style. He often browsed the newspapers for subject matter. The focus of the song was the terrible murder of a fourteen-year-old black boy in Mississippi and the subsequent mockery of a trial that exonerated his brutal killers.

Bob sings the piece in a subdued mournful voice as he tells the story of the kidnapping, torture and cold-blooded murder of the poor boy. He also highlights the civil rights issues in the Southern States where terror was a weapon used by white supremacist groups like the Ku Klux Klan and lynchings were still happening.

Perhaps the reason why the song was never properly recorded was fear that the same thing would happen to it as happened to his equally scathing attack on the KKK and right-wing white supremacy on 'Talkin' John Birch Society Blues'? Simply too controversial?

'Hero Blues' (Bob Dylan) (Unreleased)
There are two different versions of this song. The first one is a guitar version with vocal and harmonica. Then they tried it as a piano version. The guitar version has some great acoustic guitar and characteristic harmonica. The piano one has a smoother vocal but the piano plods along.

The structure of the song is a standard blues with repeating lines and humorous content. It's a thruway song about a girl who wants her man to go out and fight so she can boast to her friends about his prowess.

'Going to New Orleans' (Bob Dylan) (Freewheelin' Outtakes 2018)
Not a very crisp production on this outtake. It's a very rough copy that sounds as if it has not been fully realised yet. The strumming rolls along and the vocal and harmonica inject some urgency.

Bob is going down to New Orleans, behind the rising sun – an interesting reference to 'The House of the Rising Sun'. He's got woman problems and wants to consult the gypsy woman Marie Laveau. He's begun to realise 'My trouble has just begun'.

'(I Heard That) Lonesome Whistle' (Hank Williams, Jimmie Davis) (Freewheelin' Outtakes 2018)
The old Hank Williams song is given the Dylan treatment. Using a capo on the second fret to create a D major, he produces a dirge-like strum emblazoned with bursts of harmonica and delivers the song in a mournful moan. He's pouring out his heavy heart.

'Kingsport Town' (Traditional) (Released on The Bootleg Series 1-3)
It's not difficult to see why Bob selected this traditional song. He was missing Suze. This song summed up his feelings. She was away in sunny Italy and he was forlornly left in icy New York.

Bob's voice is full of sadness as he sings the song over a delicately picked guitar, even the harmonica is mournful and full of longing: 'I wish to my soul that I could see the girl I'm thinking of.'

'Let Me Die in My Footsteps' (Bob Dylan) (Released on The Bootleg Series 1-3)
A favourite of the bootleggers and a track that would have sat very well on the album, however, it was taken off and substituted with 'A Hard Rain's Gonna Fall'. The composition was based on a Roy Acuff song. With a capo on the first fret, it's played in the key of Ab major.

With the threat of nuclear holocaust once again the subject here, Bob threw light on the whole dilemma created by the rise of the nuclear shelter industry. Would you really deny entry into your shelter for the children next door? He refused to buy into this paranoia and saw the whole idea of shelters as doing nothing more than creating fear and division. He was of the opinion that they could be doing more positive things with their money: 'Stead of learnin' to live, they are learning to die.'

The poetic song has a smooth, haunting melody that Bob handles with a defiant melancholy air that is very reminiscent of Woody Guthrie's style. The harmonica is deployed to play the melody over a softly strummed guitar.

The song was also published by Broadside and furthermore, there is a Witmark demo. One of my favourite covers was made by Coulson, Dean, McGuinness and Flint.

'Milk Cow's Calf's Blues' (Robert Johnson) (Freewheelin' Outtakes 2018)
The song was based on the Robert Johnson version that made such an enormous impact on Bob when he was given it by John Hammond, but it goes right back in time to the early days of the blues. Kokomo Arnold made one of the early recordings of the song in 1936. There were subsequent covers by the likes of Sleepy John Estes and Skip James. It crossed over into both country and rock 'n' roll, with Elvis and Eddie Cochran producing versions.
    Bob tackles it in a traditional blues style with a picked guitar in an open E tuning with a capo on the eighth or tenth fret. He mimics the high falsetto singing at the end of verses that were used by both Arnold and Johnson.

'Quit Your Lowdown Ways' (Bob Dylan) (Released on The Bootleg Series 1-3)
Bob's feelings towards the absent Suze were vacillating between longing and anger. This is another song in that long line loosely based on Bob Will's 1940s song 'Brain Cloudy Blues'. With a double dropped D tuning and a capo on the fifth fret, Bob alternates between double and triple timing. Bob is in a cajoling mood – she needs to come home. She'll need his help someday.

'Rambling Gamblin Willie' (Bob Dylan) (Released on The Bootleg Series 1-3)
This was originally on the album and was one of the four tracks replaced following the 'Talkin' John Birch Paranoid Blues' controversy. At the time, stimulated by his publishing contract with Witmark, Bob was a veritable conveyor belt of songs. He was churning them out one after another. Not only that, but he had found a rich seam of poetic lyrics full of social content that were finding a receptive audience and getting him noticed. He was working that seam and unearthing a series of gems, each more elaborate and original than the others. In the short space of working on the album, he had come up with a number that had surpassed anything he'd written before. 'Ramblin' Gamblin' Willie' was rather derivative and more in his old Woody Guthrie style, which is probably why it had been replaced. It had already been superseded.
    The song is based on the traditional tune 'Brennan on the Moor' and played in an open D or E tuning with the capo on the eighth or tenth fret – Bob setting up a fast, jaunty strum pattern. It tells the story of a larger-than-life itinerant gambler who met his end on one of those Mississippi river boats. Willie was a Robin Hood character who always gave to the poor and needy and was shot through the head by a poor loser. Such is life.

'Rocks and Gravel' (Bob Dylan Mance Lipscomb) (Freewheelin'
Outtakes 2018, & soundtrack CD of US TV series True Detectives)
Although the writing of this is attributed to Bob, it is actually based, in
both lyrics and tune, on early blues numbers. Both Leroy Carr and Scrapper
Blackwell produced early versions under the name 'Alabama Woman Blues'.
Mance Lipscomb recorded a number called 'Rocks and Gravel Make a Solid
Road' in 1960. Bob took the early version and added a couple of verses. His
version is still in the blues style with a drop D tuning and standard finger-
picking style.

The final verse being a precursor of 'It Takes a lot to Laugh, It Takes a
Train to Cry'.

'Sally Gal' (Bob Dylan) (Freewheelin' Outtakes 2018, No Direction
Home – Bootleg Series Vol. 7)
Nothing more than a jaunty interlude. The song, which is derivative of
Woody Guthrie's 1957 'Sally Don't You Grieve', is lyrically sparse. The lyrics
state that he is gonna get this Sally gal and affirms that he is a ramblin' man.
Little more. The song starts with a long harmonica intro and sets off at quite a
pace – going nowhere. I'm not surprised it was left off the album. There's not
much to it and it's in a style that he's already left behind.

'Talkin' Bear Mountain Picnic Massacre Blues' (Bob Dylan)
(Released on The Bootleg Series 1-3)
One of Bob's party pieces. Done in the classic Woody Guthrie talking blues
style – a story told over a standard strummed, picked guitar with bursts of
harmonica between each verse. Bob liked doing these and they were always
popular in live performance.

Bob took the nub of the story out of a newspaper recounting a terrible
accident caused by unscrupulous conmen who sold far too many tickets for
a picnic boat trip, resulting in the boat becoming hopelessly overloaded and
sinking. Somehow, he turned this into a humorous piece which he would
perform with his best Chaplin-esque style. Like Guthrie, he found a way to
exaggerate, personalise and find humour in the midst of tragedy.

I'm not surprised it was left off the album. The performance was fine, but
by the time he recorded it, the song was already in his past.

'Talkin' Hava Negiliah Blues' (Bob Dylan) (Released on The Bootleg
Series 1-3)
Weighing in at under a minute, this is not so much a song as one of Bob's
jokes. The spoken intro talks of it being a foreign song he learnt in Utah.
That is obviously farcical in itself. The play is on the Jewish song 'Hava
Negiliah' and Utah being a Mormon county.

All Bob does is sing the words Hava Negiliah syllable by syllable, puts them
together at the end and finish with a cowboy yodel. It's not often we got to

hear Bob in any way referring to his Jewish roots, though.

'Walls of Red Wing' (Bob Dylan) (Released on The Bootleg Series 1-3)
Portraying the horrendous conditions in a reformatory school in Red Wing Minnesota, Bob provides graphic descriptions of the life of the young inmates and the barbaric regime that existed within the establishment and allies himself with the unfortunate inmates – reinforcing his image as a rebel in doing so.

The melody for the song comes from an old Scottish ballad entitled 'The Road and the Miles to Dundee' taught to Bob by Martin Carthy.

The song is beautifully sung to a slowly strummed guitar, interspersed with a dash of harmonica, the gorgeous melody belying the harshness of the poetic lyrics.

The song could easily have been included on the album and was much covered by other singers, including Ramblin' Jack Elliott and Joan Baez.

'Whatcha Gonna Do' (Bob Dylan) (Unreleased)
Once again, Bob claims to have written this song, but in actual fact, it is a blues number with lyrics that have been circulating in blues and spirituals since the early days of blues. There's not much original about it at all. The theme is one of death – probably not the most commercial of subjects – 'What you're gonna do when the shadow comes creepin' in your room?'. Bob plays it in open D tuning with a capo on the fifth fret and changes between straight beats and syncopated hammering to create a sombre performance, emphasised by some eerie harmonica.

'Wichita (Going To Louisiana)' (Bob Dylan) (Unreleased)
A typical Dylan song from this early period with many traditional elements. Bob knocked out a ton of these. They followed a predictable structure – Bob strumming, interspersing harmonica and telling a tale. There wasn't a great deal to it and the track was not properly produced for the album – just a rough cut.

'Worried Blues' (Hally Wood) (Released on *The Bootleg Series 1-3*)
Played on a picked 12-string guitar (a rare event) with Bob singing in a very controlled manner. A soulful delivery, all on one level, that comes out as a sad dirge but is extremely compelling nonetheless. Bob sounds world-weary well beyond his years.

'Farewell (Fare Thee Well)' (Bob Dylan)
A rare track recorded in January 1963 and loosely based on the English seafaring ballad 'The Leaving of Liverpool' that Bob had learnt while over in England. It tells the story of the protagonist venturing to California or New Mexico and leaving his girl behind. Associations with Suze and her Italian trip seem to the fore.

The Times They Are A-Changin' (1964)

Personnel:
Bob Dylan: acoustic guitar, piano, vocals and harmonica
Tom Wilson: producer
Label: Colombia
Recorded at Colombia Studio A
Release date: February 1964
Highest chart positions: UK: 4 US: 20

This was the first album to feature just Bob Dylan songs. Not a single cover.

1964 was a bittersweet time for Bob. His career was rocketing. The year started with Suze away on a prolonged trip that she kept extending and his relationship with Joan Baez was developing. The relationship with Joan developed into a full-blown affair and the relationship with Suze broke down. It was a time of confusion, sorrow and delight. There were a lot of claims on his time and emotions. He was playing before large crowds. Success loomed. In 1963, Bob had appeared for the first time at the Newport Festival before a crowd of thousands and had gone down well. In 1964, he had become a star and dominated the festival. He was lauded by the whole folk establishment and even eclipsed Joan Baez.

On top of that, the influence of Albert Grossman, which was a tad paranoid, the strained relations with some of his peers (who resented his sudden success), the distance from his easy-going relationship with his initial small audiences, and the constant pressure from the media was beginning to have an effect. He began putting up defences, creating a persona to hide behind.

The influence of Woody Guthrie was still very much apparent in both the content and the cover photo. Dylan was still producing songs that told a story. He was turning to newspaper headlines for inspiration in the way that Woody had. These were stories straight out of the civil rights movement; tales of racism, exploitation and hardship. There were songs about equality, war and anger. What was missing was the humour. Where before, in both live performance and on record, Dylan had presented a Chaplin-esque humour to lighten the message, these songs were much starker and more sombre. Was the break-up with Suze taking its toll? Was the pressure beginning to mount?

Whatever the reasons for the change, there was no doubting that Dylan was beginning to take off in a big way. Mutt's prediction had come true. This second single was a surprising Top Ten hit. For the first time, a raw folk song with a topical message and simple arrangement had broken through into the mainstream charts. In fact, on the whole, the album does away with the electric, instrumental experimentation from the previous album in favour of raw, stripped-back folk here. Probably the sober nature of the material did not lend itself to an upbeat backing.

As a fifteen-year-old rebel, I remember sitting on the bed with Mutt listening to 'The Times They Are A-Changin'' and thinking that the song spoke for me. It was a clarion call for a generation of change, a change of sensitivities – the most positive track on the album. Jingoistic it might have been, but it drew us in. It made us feel we were part of a new movement and that was the entry point to the rest of the album with its dire social messaging, poetic lyrics and anger. Even though our lives in the Thames Delta were thousands of miles away from the slavery of the Deep South of America, Bob painted the pictures so that we could feel the injustice. We had already lived through the Cuban Missile Crisis so we understood the shadow of a nuclear holocaust. As young white kids, we were open to grasping the content of the album.

As with *Freewheelin'*, Bob was pushing an agenda of social consciousness, taking Woody's message forward. His intimate stories of families in crisis were highlighting the plights of millions. His stories of racism were emphasising the reality of civil rights. His anti-war polemics were questioning how the world was being run and power deployed. Whether he intended it or not, liked it or not, his songs were impacting massively on young people. Bob might have seen himself as competing with his fellow singer-songwriters, trying to make an impact, trying to break through, trying to outdo them all, but his songs were hitting on a wider stage and raising the awareness of youth across the globe. He lived in the bohemian bubble of Greenwich Village, but that cosy world was already being blown apart. Perhaps unknowingly, or simply at a level beyond his belief, his songs were being analysed, dissected and were raising awareness, activating sensitivities and encouraging young people to question. Even the organs of the establishment were beginning to pay attention. They recognised there was more to this. He was being talked of as a 'serious' poet. These were developments that were beyond his wildest expectations, scary, pressure-loading, threatening and fast-growing to a level that was out of control.

This was an album full of passion, incandescence and controlled anger. Bob now had the power to do what he wanted and vented his fury, no longer afraid to name names. This was an album that set out to change the world. Dylan was not holding back.

'The Times They Are A-Changin'' (Bob Dylan)

Having now secured his position as a prominent writer of topical songs and established his reputation, Bob deliberately sought to cement his position. He set out to write an anthem reflecting this new age of change sweeping the western hemisphere. He used the Irish and Scottish ballads 'Come All Ye Bold Highway Men' and 'Come All Ye Tender Hearted Maidens' as the melody and wrote a set of lyrics that reflected what was happening in society.

The early sixties represented an explosion of expression and culture. It felt as if the shackles of the war years and its subsequent years of austerity with its grey conservatism and conformity were finally being shaken loose. There was a new way of looking at the world, a new morality, a new wave of liberalism and it was sweeping all before it. Bob felt himself to be at the forefront of this revolution. We'd had the beatniks and rock 'n' roll and now it was all coming together. A new age was being born. Bob set out to chronicle its inception. He was rocketing forward, spearheading this new philosophy.

Perhaps, unwittingly, this was the start of his inception as the voice of a generation – a media-generated epithet that he would soon come to despise and regret. But he had brought it upon himself. He captured the moment so perfectly:

And don't criticize
What you can't understand
Your sons and your daughters
Are beyond your command
Your old road is rapidly agin
Please get out of the new one
If you can't lend your hand
For the times they are a-changin'

The irony is that within a few years, Bob would find himself appalled by this new age and as out of touch with it as any of the old guard.

This was one of the songs that acted as a battle cry for the new generation. They took up the anthem, took up his message of change, took on the philosophy of civil rights and anti-war and married it to the new hedonism. Over the next few years, Bob embraced that hedonism, the drugs, sex and rock 'n' roll. But it was all going to implode for him.

At this point in time, he craved the attention, was still striving for fame and recognition and basking in the success. This anthem was released as a single in the UK and made the Top Ten, just like my mate Mutt had prophesised. What a revelation that was! Bob had taken the obscure, niche music of folk into mainstream pop. This was extraordinary and groundbreaking.

Musically there is nothing exceptional about the song. The clarity of the singing strings based around that G chord were a simple strum. There was no other backing and Bob used his soulful harmonica as a bridge to separate the verses. What made it special was the melodic verses sung by Bob with its memorable rousing words. It was a wall-shaking anthem that was destined to be picked up by band after band. He'd achieved his aim of producing an anthem that reflected the times.

'Please get out of the new one if you can't lend a hand' still makes me wonder what things might have been like if Bob had later embraced the philosophy he was espousing instead of abandoning it. The times changed and left him behind.

'Ballad of Hollis Brown' (Bob Dylan)
Bob took the chords and tune from the Appalachian song 'Pretty Polly' that

he had played earlier in Greenwich Village. This time he used a sombre, doom-laden flat-picking style with a double dropped D tuning and a capo on the first fret.

Through eleven verses, the poetic lyrics tell the sad story of a poor sharecropping South Dakota farmer who gets into dire straits as a result of the poverty and hardship his family face. There's no help to be found. In desperation, he kills his starving kids and wife before turning the gun upon himself. Told in second person present tense, the drama is electric as the woeful tale unfurls, and disaster after disaster befalls the family. The tension builds as their circumstances become more and more fraught. The pressure becoming unbearable.

The song is taking Woody Guthrie's storytelling and social commentary to a new level.

'With God on Our Side' (Bob Dylan)

Bob was really getting in his stride with these long poetic epics. For the most part, he was selecting a melody from an established song, usually a traditional folk song, and grafting on his own lyrics. In this case, the tune was based on an Irish folk song, 'The Merry Month of May'. This had already been used by Dominic Behan in his song 'The Patriot Game'. Dylan's opening verse was also very similar to Behan's second verse which led to some altercations.

From the narrow focus of a single tragic farming family, we're swept into the broad canvas of the whole of American history – a catalogue of wars. From the genocide of the Native Americans, the Spanish/Mexican war, through the civil war, the First World War, and Second World War to the 1960s anti-communist cold war with Russia and its threat of nuclear holocaust.

The irony was that all this death, hatred and violence was supposedly condoned by God himself. As Bob says: 'You never ask questions with God on your side.' But Bob was asking questions. He was suggesting that no God could ever condone this carnage. After singing about the weapons of chemical dust, he ends by saying, 'If God's on our side, he'll stop the next war.' Like many of Bob's new lyrics, the song took the high moral ground and was designed to make people think.

'One Too Many Mornings' (Bob Dylan)

A beautifully crafted song sung wistfully to a gently picked guitar. The open A tuning with capo on the third fret creates a sadness that is reflected by the melancholy harmonica playing and a vocal that is tinged with loss.

Bob is alone in his room, listening to the sounds of the night and reflecting on his lost love a thousand miles away, their differences and bickering.

'North Country Blues' (Bob Dylan)

After the lilting love song, we are treated to another melancholy offering sung simply in the Woody Guthrie manner. Through ten rhyming verses, this intimate tale in the first person tells of the shutting of an iron ore mine and its subsequent devastating effect on a family, the hard-working father turning to drink in his despair. As we progress through the song, we find that the narrator is the wife.

The simplicity of the rendition, based around the strumming of two repeated chords coupled with Bob's deadpan delivery, serves to enhance the hopelessness of the situation.

As with 'The Ballad of Hollis Brown', the homing in on one small story against the backdrop of a bigger social tragedy serves to highlight the human impact. Dylan has picked up where Woody left off and made these social documentaries his own. This is all the more poignant when considering the iron ore town of Hibbing where Bob was brought up.

'Only a Pawn in Their Game' (Bob Dylan)

A political song written following the murder of the civil rights activist Medgar Evers. Where other singers wrote songs directly about Medgar, Dylan chose to point the finger at the Southern populist politicians who stir up support for their election by using the race card. He accused them of using racist rhetoric to gain votes and in so doing, unleashing the fear and hatred that results in violence and murder. The cowardly assassin was no more than a pawn, exploited, brainwashed and set off like a guided missile. The real culprits were the politicians and media who stoked the fires of hate for their own ends. It was a different and powerful angle. Because it wasn't tied into any one incident, it was all the more potent.

The quiet strumming in the key of A major with a capo on the 2nd fret, starkly sets off Bob's insistent lyrics as he spills the rhyming words in a torrent, accentuating the power of the poetry. There is real intensity in the delivery as Bob barks and snarls with great clarity of annunciation. He wanted the message heard and understood.

'Boots of Spanish Leather' (Bob Dylan)

The song takes the form of an exchange of letters between the two lovers. The subject of Bob's correspondence is, of course, Suze Rotolo, who is over in Italy on a prolonged study. The separation is a torment for Bob and his frustration is evident. The lyrics eloquently capture all the sadness as he realises from her reactions that their love affair is over. She doesn't care enough.

The forlorn jilted love is amply reflected in the heart-breaking tones of Bob's singing. The melody is a slower version of the English folk song 'Scarborough Fair' as taught to Bob by Martin Carthy.

'When the Ship Comes In' (Bob Dylan)

Following the sweet, sad refrain of the end of a glorious love affair, we are straight into the vitriol and venom of revenge. It seems that in 1963 when

Bob was relatively unknown and just starting to tour with Joan Baez, he was refused entry into a hotel because of his scruffy appearance. Joan had to vouch for him. In a fit of pique, he scrawled out the song.

Bob had been much taken with the work of Berthold Brecht and particularly the song 'Pirate Jenny' from Kurt Weill's *Threepenny Opera*. Suze had been working in the production staff at The Circle In The Square Theatre putting on the Brecht play and Bob, who regularly dropped in to see Suze, had watched numerous performances and become obsessed. He dissected the song to look at its structure and what makes it work. In the song, Pirate Jenny dreams of a ship that will come and destroy all her enemies. Bob deployed the same theme. In Bob's version, the ship comes in and all his enemies are conquered.

The song can be viewed in a number of ways. In one sense, it is Bob taking his revenge on the desk clerk who refused him entry. In a wider context, it is the social underdogs gaining revenge over all the forces that are keeping them down – the ship is some kind of social revolution.

The song belts along as Bob strums and snarls his rhetoric. He crows his victorious anthem in one long angry rain of contempt.

'The Lonesome Death of Hattie Carroll' (Bob Dylan)

This song is another of Bob's topical songs written in his reporting style based on a newspaper story. Once again, he was using a single incident to illustrate wider issues. In this case, these were racism and inequality. The melody is largely taken from a folk song called 'Mary Hamilton'.

The story is based on an incident where it was reported that a wealthy aristocrat by the name of William Zantzinger, in a fit of pique, struck out with his cane at a 51-year-old black kitchen maid by the name of Hattie Carrol, and killed her. Zantzinger showed no remorse and, despite assurance by the judge that all people would be treated equally, was sentenced to a mere six months.

By focusing on this one incident, he was highlighting the inherent racism and inequality prevalent in society.

'Restless Farewell' (Bob Dylan)

'Restless Farewell' has a melody based on the traditional Irish-Scots ballad 'The Parting Glass'.

A great choice to end the album. The brisk guitar strumming is based around the chords of C, G and D and is accompanied by a mournful-sounding harmonica. The lyrics are full of nostalgia and longing as Bob looks back at friends, lovers and causes, but has no regrets for any of it. He gave to them all wholeheartedly. His voice is laden with sadness and passion, but it's time to move on to other things. In the morning, he'll be gone. There may be regret in leaving everything behind, but there is the promise of a new start. In the end, it is a positive song. It is both a full stop and a new paragraph, perhaps a whole new chapter. Are the friends the fellow singers in the village? Is he thinking of Suze when he talks of lovers? Are the causes the civil rights and anti-war movements?

Even as we finish this album laden with barbed social comment, Bob is indicating that the next will have a new direction.

Outtakes
'Paths of Victory' (Bob Dylan) (Released on The Bootleg Series 1-3)
A piano song using the chords B, E and F major – reminds me of one of those old spirituals that were used to good effect in the civil rights movement. The harmonica is jaunty and the piano bangs away in a solid rhythm. The lyrics tell of a positive message that is a clarion call to take up arms against injustice. There will be rough times ahead, but we shall fight, persevere and we will be victorious. Reminds me of the old 1930s union songs.

> Tha mornin' train was movin'
> The hummin' of its wheels
> Told me of a new day comin' across the field
> Trails of troubles
> Roads of battles
> Paths of victory
> We shall walk

Perhaps a little too optimistic for the timbre of the album?

'Moonshiner' (Traditional – arranged by Bob Dylan) (Released on *The Bootleg Series 1-3*)
A traditional song also known as 'Moonshine Blues', 'The Bottle Song' or 'Kentucky Moonshiner'.

Dylan plucks the strings in standard finger-picking style with a capo on the fourth fret in the key of C minor to create a solid base over which he plays a melancholy harmonica and sings in a voice full of sadness. The result is a mournful tale that sounds like a dirge as it tells the story of a social outsider, a moonshiner, who has lived his simple life outside the law, free and easy, and nearing the end, is now looking back.

Another of life's outcasts that Bob was identifying with during this early Guthrie period.

'Only a Hobo' (Bob Dylan) (Released on *The Bootleg Series 1-3*)
Another C, G, D chord structure with a simple arrangement, so much like Guthrie you could think that he wrote it. Even the theme, identifying with the hobos who roamed the country, riding the blinds and working for food, is reminiscent of Woody. Bob is reminding us all that even those that have reached the bottom, who, for reasons unknown, find themselves destitute,

are real people with a story to tell. Bob turns a tragic lonesome death on the streets into a moral lesson about homelessness and the poor and needy.

> Does it take much of a man to see his whole life go down
> To look up on the world from a hole in the ground
> To wait for your future like a horse that's gone lame
> To lie in the gutter and die with no name?

'Seven Curses' (Bob Dylan)

If you did not know that Bob had written this, you would think that it is a traditional folk song. There are a number of aspects that give it a Dylan twist, such as the half-rhymes that he deploys and the feeling of sadness he creates with the wonderful melody. The guitar, tuned to a dropped D with a capo on the second fret, echoes the bleakness of the story. It chimes and rings as Bob plucks the beauty out of it.

In contrast with such beauty, this horrid tale of power, lust and betrayal is similar to that of 'Gallows Pole' (Leadbelly sung it as 'Gallis Pole'). Bob puts his slant on it and sings it with great intensity. Every line unfurls the story and propels it forward towards the terrible betrayal, followed by those dreadful curses.

'Percy's Song' (Bob Dylan to a traditional melody) (Released on *Biograph*)

Once again, Bob uses a traditional melody to lay his words on. In this instance, it is 'The Wind and the Rain' which was derived from 'The Two Sisters'. In many ways, the tale is similar to that of 'Seven Curses'. Bob is outlining a miscarriage of justice and one's impotency against the law of the land. The story follows his attempts to plead the case of one of his friends who has committed a crime and received a draconian sentence.

In the key of D major with a capo on the second fret, Bob lays down a delicately plucked bed of notes over which he soulfully intones his sorrowful tale in a lilting, gentle tenor.

'Lay Down Your Weary Tune' (Bob Dylan) (Released on Biograph)

A melody that eats its way through your ears into your brain and echoes around your skull – so beautiful that it refuses to leave. You find yourself unconsciously singing it while you are busy. The beauty doesn't stop with the melody; the poetic lyrics are just as evocative. The key of A major, with chords A, D and E major, gives it a real lift as Bob's lilting voice describes the mystical elements of nature and music. He likens the sounds around him to musical instruments, as if Mother Nature is sounding a joyful symphony of transcendent joy in which we can all be healed.

He wrote it at Joan Baez's house in Carmel. I always imagine him sitting under a tree strumming these delicate chords while lost in the wonders of the universe around him.

Much too upward to fit with the more sombre mood of the album.

'Eternal Circle' (Bob Dylan) (Released on The Bootleg Series 1-3)
The song is based around a simple recurring, jaunty guitar pattern in the key of C major, running around the chords C, F and G major with a capo on the third fret.

I have spoken to a number of musicians who have iterated the theme of this song – the power of music (and a musician) to form and sense the sexual bond that flows between the performer and a member of the audience: 'Through a bullet of light her face was reflectin' the fast fading words that rolled from my tongue'. The force of the music and the personality can make a two-way electric connection.

In this case, the singer is aware of the rapt attention he has created and is similarly affected. He tries to blot her out and complete the song. Looking over at the end, he finds that the girl has left and resignedly moves on to the next song.

'Suze (The Cough Song)' (Bob Dylan) (Released on The Bootleg Series 1-3)
A wonderful fluid instrumental – the first instrumental that Bob had attempted. The fingerpicking is sharp and crisp, notes delicately ringing with the clarity of the positioning as Bob moves through some really brisk chord changes: C to F to C to G with a D and an A thrown into the mix. With the capo on the fourth fret, it makes for a delightful swinging sound.

The muse for this song was Suze, his girlfriend at the time. The two were deeply in love. When she became pregnant, after much soul searching, aware of the difficulties prevalent in their ages and relationship, she chose to have an abortion. Bob's ongoing relationship with Joan Baez was the final shutting of the door and they split up shortly after.

The tune later mutated into 'Nashville Skyline Rag' and was released on the *Nashville Skyline* album.

The reason it is subtitled 'The Cough Song' is because Bob broke out into a fit of coughing before the end of the song, causing Bob to stop playing as he proclaimed it was the end of the song – that it should fade out just before he starts coughing. Tom Wilson, his producer, chuckles and agrees.

'New Orleans Rag' (Bob Dylan) (Released on The 50th Anniversary Collection)
To perform this song, Bob put a capo on the third fret. The tune is based around the chords G, D7 and C. He also performed it as a piano piece.

Bob liked to pepper his concerts with humorous songs that he could do with his Chaplin routine. They lightened the atmosphere and provided balance. This number, sung in the first person, finds Bob feeling very down.

A friend recommends he visit this lady of repute who could fix him up good. He's just about to knock on her door when he spies a series of wrecked individuals crawling, groaning, muttering, shuffling out of that place looking like they'd been wrecked with a monkey wrench. Scared silly, he backs away and makes a run for it.

I doubt that many singers have made such a comical story out of a prostitute. It certainly succeeds in raising a laugh, but it was obvious that it did not suit the tone of the album.

Medley 'That's Alright' (Arthur 'Big Boy' Crudup) / **'Sally Free and Easy'** (Cyril Tawney) (Released on The 50th Anniversary Collection)
'That's Alright' was the Arthur Crudup number. Interestingly, this shows that in 1963 Bob was still thinking about rock 'n' roll and Elvis Presley, who made a rockabilly hit out of this country blues number. 'Sally Free and Easy' was the Cyril Tawney number written in 1958 that Bob picked up when over in London.

'East Laredo Blues' (Bob Dylan) (Released on The 50th Anniversary Collection)
Based around a jangly piano creating a Tex-Mex sound. The instrumental goes on and on without a lot to offer. Sounds like a mess around in the studio – nothing more.

'Hero Blues' (Bob Dylan) (Released on *The 50th Anniversary Collection*)
Another attempt at recording this song. This one featured Bob, his guitar and harmonica and sounds complete. Another humorous song that simply does not fit in with the mood of the album.

Singles:
'Times They Are A-Changin' b/w **'Honey, Just allow Me One More Chance'** (from Freewheelin') (UK)
This track has an immense importance as being a breakthrough single, not only for Bob but also for 'serious' pop music. It was released in the UK though strangely not in the USA. Bob wrote it as an epic, anthemic song and that it was; cementing the new consciousness, civil rights, antiwar and new youth culture together in one package and acting as a clarion call to young people. They rose up in numbers to embrace it. Despite only reaching number nine in the charts, it was remarkable and had a far bigger impact than its sales or chart position suggested. This was the song that set the tone. Not only did it smash down barriers by launching a raw acoustic track into the pop charts, but was also the first of what was called 'protest' songs by the media. While Dylan hated the term, it did indicate that we were now dealing with songs that had content and meaning – a move away from the trite love songs that tended to be the sum total of pop singers' output. This was the

single that heralded a new era.

As to whether Bob was being passionate and genuine, we'll never know. Was he really under the thrall of Suze Rotollo? Was he caught up in the passion of the folk scene and its close alliance, at that time, with these left-wing values? Or was he merely being cynical, seeing an opportunity and jumping into the gap? We all know how later, when he wanted to move out from under this 'label' he had landed himself with; he called himself 'Just a song and dance man' and his reply when Tony Glover asked him what this shit was all about was 'Well, you know, it seems to be what the people want to hear.'

Not that it matters. The song stands on its own. It had the effect, whether the sentiments were genuine or feigned.

Another Side of Bob Dylan (1964)

Personnel:
Bob Dylan: acoustic guitar, piano, vocals and harmonica
Tom Wilson: producer
Label: Colombia
Recorded at Colombia Studio A
Release date: August 1964
Highest chart positions: UK: 8 US: 43

By now, Bob Dylan was a mainstream success. He was reported in serious newspapers. His lyrics were analysed. In some circles, they spoke of him as a poet. Even as The Beatles broke in America, Bob Dylan had started the task of dragging 'pop music' into an art form that could be appreciated by adults. It was nothing short of a revolution. Rock 'n' roll had created a visceral revolution and now Dylan was, almost single-handedly, making that revolution cerebral. Before long, the poetic lyrics of Dylan, with its social message, were about to get married to the power of rock to create a new hybrid that was going to blossom in the late sixties as the counter-cultural revolution took off.

The whole album was overshadowed by Bob's split with Suze. Her influence was missing. Without her clear-cut vision, Bob was becoming increasingly disillusioned. He was seeing everything as being much more complex. Nothing was black and white: 'What's wrong goes much deeper than the bomb'.

Although his sensibilities were still very much with the underdog – he was still rooting for civil rights and against war – he was not seeing any solutions. What was wrong with society was systemic. He refused to be confined to the views of any movement, he felt that was too restricting. The reality of this was brought home to him when he agreed to accept the Tom Paine Award from The Emergency Civil Liberties Committee. This is what Bob said about the event from an interview with *The New Yorker*:

> Here were all these people who had supported the left in the thirties. Now they were supporting civil rights drives. That's groovy. But they also had minks and jewels, and it was like they were giving money out of guilt – a bunch of people who had nothing to do with my kind of politics.

He got scared, drank too much, tried to leave and ended up giving a rambling speech in which he attempted to explain his complex position, made some inflammatory statements and was roundly booed.

There was much going on in Dylan's life that was having an effect on Bob's music. He had discovered the French poet Rimbaud and was excitedly extolling the virtues of his dense poetic imagery and themes, even telling friends that this was the type of poetry he intended to be writing from then on. There was then Dylan's affair with Joan Baez and the consequent breakdown of his relationship with Suze, previously outlined. Following the painful split with Suze, Bob went on a European tour, playing in England before going on to Paris. In Paris, he met the German model Nico who was later going to move to New York and become part of Andy Warhol's entourage, making films with him and becoming part of The Velvet Underground. Mixed in with all this emotion and turmoil, Bob had his first introduction to psychedelics in the form of LSD. The drug mix of LSD and marijuana would impact on his writing, as would the arrival of The Beatles. Suze had been hugely affected by The Beatles and reports of Bob's reaction to them ranged from him calling their music 'bubblegum' to pulling the car over to listen and enthuse. He thought their chords and harmonies were outrageous. This was the year that he was to meet up with John, Paul, George and Ringo, and begin a relationship that would cross-pollinate all their lives and future musical development.

Added to all this was Bob's burgeoning fame, the impact of which was creating enormous pressure to keep coming up with the goods. Fame was creating a tiring touring commitment, a need to constantly produce new material of a consistently high standard, peripherals such as radio and TV appearances, interviews and a contract to produce a novel – the frustrations of writing *Tarantula* is something that would dog his life for years. Albert Grossman was keen to seize every opportunity and push Bob into doing more and more.

The result of all this upheaval was that the music and poetry changed. After the rather stark social commentary of *The Times They Are A-Changin'*, this album is more personal and biographical. A number of the songs are dealing with the painful split with Suze, others, like 'Chimes of Freedom' and 'To Ramona' still have that backbone of deep social concern and identification with the underdog, but this time imbued with more Rimbaudian poetic imagery and less finger pointing.

While the album had an underlying sadness that pervaded the songs, it also contained a defiance and even a return to that earlier humour. What comes over is that Bob is torn over the loss of his great love, he wants her back but, at the same time, is determined to move on.

Musically the album is quite simple. Most of the songs are played in G or C major, with the occasional use of a capo. There is one piano piece. There are a few chord changes that are deployed such as the move from G to G6 and G7.

This is the last of Bob's series of three acoustic gems from the sixties. Although half of the next album *Bringing it All Back Home* is acoustic, the predominant feel is that the album is electric. Even though this album has a number of Bob's early acoustic masterpieces, for which the folk cognoscenti rightly lauded him, it also heralds a big departure in style and content that augers a move away from that scene. The strictures of the folk movement were proving too restricting with its forceful allying to clearcut left-wing values. Bob was seeing things more complexly. Bob no longer felt able to draw up distinct lines. He was about to develop into different arenas that would create a huge tempest in his wake. The folk brigade thought that he no longer supported the struggle for civil rights or cared about war, racism and poverty. They felt let down. Not that Bob cared. Wilfully he always did exactly what he wanted and refused to be diverted.

Incredibly, the whole album was recorded in one mammoth eight-hour session! That must rate up there with the Beatles recording their first album as a major achievement.

'All I Really Want to Do' (Bob Dylan)

It is as if in this song, with its joyful humour and playful lyrics, Bob is feeling the need to reassert his philosophy. He does not want to point fingers, apportion blame, categorise or put people down – he just wants to be friends. Well, he said he was just a 'song-and-dance' man, didn't he? All he wanted to do was entertain.

The song has an upward feel due to its A major key with the capo on the second fret. Bob sings the song's title at the end of each verse in a Hank Williams-style yodel that is very effective, adding a breezy lightness.

In many ways, the song is making fun of his own serious songs. He certainly finds it all amusing as can be heard with the amused chuckles he inserts as if the very thought of trying to influence other peoples' minds on serious issues is simply preposterous. On another level, it is a song aimed at trying to reassure (a girl) that he has no intentions to convert or overwhelm her with his own ideology. He disingenuously just wants to be friends – remembering that the young Bob was a wicked, wanton womaniser.

The track proved very popular, being covered numerous times and simultaneously charting at the time for both The Byrds and Cher.

'Black Crow Blues' (Bob Dylan)

This is unusual for this point in time; the first we hear of Dylan accompanying himself on piano, creating a rhythmic set of simple chords in an unrefined blues style that is nonetheless effective.

The lyrics create a picture of a lonesome Dylan standing on a country road, trying to thumb a ride. He has no watch but nervously feels the passing of time as he fails to get anywhere. He's bereft, missing his lost girl. She can come back to him anytime. One minute he's feeling invincible, but the next he's just flat down. He's feeling so miserable that he can't even scare the crows away. Suze is the muse, but it's not one of the best to come out of this sorrowful split.

'Spanish Harlem Incident' (Bob Dylan)

Having moved away from basing his songs on existing traditional melodies, we find Bob producing a superb haunting tune that makes the track. Even though the guitar is playing a simple C, D, G riff, the vocal, augmented by some characteristic harmonica, is soaring into a mesmerising refrain that is completely captivating. The rises in the voice propel it along.

Who is this mysteriously seductive girl that has captivated him? A dark-skinned gypsy lass with flashing eyes and pearly teeth, who appeared, passed and was gone as Bob made his way through Spanish Harlem? Or was this dusky beauty Joan or Suze?

Whoever it was, she certainly made an impression that brought out the best of Bob's poetic spirit. She's 'too hot for taming', what with all those 'flaming feet' and the 'rattling drums', of his own heart, his 'restless palms' demand to know if their future is together as he is under the power of her 'flashing diamond teeth' and 'wildcat charms'. Bob is drowning. He doesn't know who he is anymore. She's so sublime – is he dreaming? Is he dead?

'Chimes of Freedom' (Bob Dylan)

For me, there are three stand-out songs on this album and this is the first. A Bob Dylan masterpiece – one of the songs still influenced by Suze and the sensibilities that she engendered in Bob. Here he is identifying strongly with all the downtrodden and outcasts of society. He and his companion are sheltering from a storm and experiencing a mystical epiphany as the heavens put on an extravagant display of wonder and awe. The skies rip open with a torrential downpour, accompanied by crashing thunder and great flashes of lightning that send the whole world into a glorious display that put our puny fireworks to shame. This is no spectacle for the wealthy, nature (god) is creating an uplifting performance of might, majesty and spell-binding beauty for the poor, all those oppressed and abused.

While this is not a finger-pointing song, it is one that strongly allies with all those people so hard-pressed. This show is just for them. From their shelter, Bob and his companion watch awestruck, moved and stunned as the universe performs. The sounds of spiritual church wedding bells blend with the primaeval spirituality of the thunder to create a transcendental concoction for the transfixed observers. He imagines that the bells and thunder are tolling for the wretched.

The starting point for the song lies in an old nineteenth-century ballad called 'The Bells of Trinity' in which the lyrics 'tolling for the outcast, tolling for the gay' and 'we listened to the chimes of Trinity' feature. Dave Van Ronk played the song to Bob having learnt it from his grandmother. Bob composed his own song inspired by 'The Bells of Trinity' while on a road trip across America with Paul Clayton, Pete Karman and Victor Maimudes. The lyrics are soaked in Rimbaud imagery and were further inspired by a moving meeting with civil rights activists Bernice Johnson and Cordell Reagon. The flame of justice still burned. The end result is a tour de force of social indictment. The dregs of society who had been discarded were being lauded. They weren't worthless. The simple guitar accompaniment, based around the chords G, C and D, was a base for the adornment of a poetic wonder. The eloquence and spectacular delivery lifted it into a world of its own.

In 1988 Bruce Springsteen carried out a tour in aid of Amnesty International (along with Sting and Tracy Chapman) in which he sang the song with a riveting spoken introduction. It was released as part of an EP, with proceeds going to Amnesty International. In 2012, Bob endorsed the release of a four-CD compilation in aid of Amnesty International entitled *Chimes of Freedom: The Songs of Bob Dylan Honouring 50 Years of Amnesty International* which included this 1964 song.

'I Shall Be Free No. 10' (Bob Dylan)

In line with the lighter tone of this album, Bob thought it was appropriate to add one of his humorous pieces. This sprightly little song zings along and always brings out a chuckle, yet it still has, like most of his comic numbers, content worthy of dissection.

Within this jolly lyric, there are some playful touches, such as the way he pokes fun at Cassius Clay (Muhammed Ali) and the way Cassius used to ham it up with his poetic predictions, but there were also a lot of serious jibes disguised in jest. It begins with Bob trying to undermine the perception of him being a serious poet/spokesperson: 'It ain't no use a-talking to me. It's just the same as talking to you.' He goes on through many stanzas to obliquely touch on McCarthy's manufactured red scare, imagining the Russians getting up to heaven first, before moving on to liberalism, stating that 'I'm liberal to a degree', but he wouldn't allow his daughter to marry the ultra-right Barry Goldwater 'for all the farms in Cuba'. He then mocks the absurdity of pop music dance trends and fashion, before taking a swipe at all his two-faced folk friends who now hate him for his fame and success. Finally, he winds up having a go at the establishment who take his poetry seriously and the intolerance of conservative America. The last verse, mentioning his guitar playing as 'just something I learned over in England', is a jab at those who were having a go at him for 'stealing' the melodies from traditional songs.

There are a number of serious matters that can be touched upon within the bubble of comedy, aided by four chords and a cheery harmonica.

'To Ramona' (Bob Dylan)

For me, this is the second major gem on the album, a song so full of sentiment that it never fails to move me. The melody may be based on the Mexican El Corrido folk tradition and it may well be also based on the 1937 country classic 'The Last Letter' by Rex Griffin, but the poetic beauty of the track, the soothing sensitive performance, edged with such concern, makes this, for me, one of Bob's outstanding tracks.

The song takes the form of a letter to a lover, a girl from the country who is finding the city and her friends' backbiting all too much, who is suffering greatly, extremely upset and looking to go back home to the South. I always imagined this lover as being black, a personal view taken from the snatches of lyrics: 'As to be by the strength of your skin' and 'returnin' back to the South', but Joan Baez claims that it was written about her. Bob was in a relationship with Nico at the time, so it could be about anyone and no one. As he will not say, it is anybody's guess. Bob is comforting her, assuring her that she has worth, should believe in herself and to take no notice of vicious fools that surround her: 'an' there's no use in tryin' to deal with the dyin''.

The comfort he is offering is also pertinent to himself. At this time, he was struggling with fame and having to deal with the two-faced viciousness stemming from former friends who were jealous of his success. There was pertinence to the lyrics:

You know you got
Nothing to win and nothing to lose
From fixtures and forces and friends
Your sorrow does stem
That hype you and type you
Making you feel
That you gotta be just like them

Bob ends by telling her that 'Everything passes, everything changes, just do what you think you should do.'

The song, resonating with those harmonic motifs of the G, G6, G7 chords that he uses so much on the album, is sung with such tenderness and sincerity, using such poetic imagery that it never fails to touch the heart. It paints the picture of the two of them battling it out against a cruel world of heartless fools and yet holds on to that thread of optimism.

'Motorpsycho Nitemare' (Bob Dylan)

Straight from the sublime to the absurd in this amusing poetic narrative that uses the Hitchcock film *Psycho* as the basis of the story.

To a strummed guitar simply moving from G, C to D, Bob takes us through the tale. He positions himself as a travelling salesman/doctor who stops at an isolated farm to ask for a room for the night – the farmers in the mid-West being notoriously ultra-right-wing. The farmer agrees as long as he milks the cow in the morning and stays away from his daughter. In the night, the daughter appears and wants him to take a shower. Bob is hip to the slashing shower scene horror show and somehow makes his getaway by shouting out, 'I like Fidel Castro and his beard' which incensed the anti-commie farmer and extricated Bob from his obligation to milk the cow. He departs rapidly as the farmer lets fly at him with his shotgun. The humorous parting line of the song being 'Without freedom of speech I might be in the swamp', an oblique reference to the civil rights campaigners Goodman, Schwerner and Chaney, who were murdered and thrown into a swamp by racist ultra-right-wingers.

'My Back Pages' (Bob Dylan)

This is the third genius song and is crucial in understanding the change that had taken place in Bob. If age is supposed to bring wisdom and understanding, then Bob is saying that he's far less sure now than he ever was. It is as if his old self-assured self was older than this new self who was racked with doubts and saw these issues as hugely complicated: 'Good and bad, I define these terms, quite clear, no doubt, somehow. Ah, but I was so much older then, I'm younger than that now'.

The split with Suze had left him unsure. Where, in his younger days he had seen everything clearly, everything looked much more complicated now. Issues of war and civil rights were not as simple as he had previously seen them. He could no longer voice the same vehement arguments and take the same extreme stances. Hence his poetry had veered away from the angry, finger-pointing and moved towards more personal issues even though the social concerns were there enveloped within these more introspective songs.

This doubt led to a general disillusionment with the whole protest movement. He now saw it as far too one-dimensional – he was trying for something more nuanced.

The irony is that the song is sung and played in the same style as deployed on the last album, *The Times They Are A-Changin'*, and carries that same mournful melody and vibe, yet, at the same time, what it is suggesting is a complete break with what has gone before. It started life under the title 'Ancient Memories', which suggests that Bob was already feeling a million miles away from the sentiments he had previously expressed such a short time before. Loosely based on the traditional folk song 'Young But Growing', Bob has turned it into a deeply poetic offering in which the complex lyrics are open to interpretation, tantalisingly clear but yet ambiguous. The genius lies in the poetry married to the melody.

'I Don't Believe You' (Bob Dylan)

A complex strum on the guitar mainly based around the C, G and G7 chords leads us into what comes across as a light, cheery uplifting melody. Bob's vocal delivery is in the same vein – one of amused disbelief. How could this girl, who he had been so close to, simply pretend that the two of them have never had a romantic connection? As he struggles with his bemusement, he keeps his heartache hidden behind a curtain of light-heartedness and resignation. The bluesy, interspersed harmonica is brilliantly at odds with the guitar vibe but adds to the overall impact. There is a chuckle from Bob as he realises that he has mixed up the verses. The whole of this album was recorded in one session and a number of the tracks in one take. They must have decided that the chuckle added to the overall tone of the song and the mixed-up lyrics did not matter.

In later performances of this song ('I Don't Believe You (She Acts Like We Never Have Met')), it has a much darker vibe and the hurt shows through.

Another song that owes its muse to the tragic break-up between Bob and Suze.

'Ballad in Plain D' (Bob Dylan)

The title is a slight misnomer; the guitar is tuned to C with a capo on the second fret, which does transform it into the key of D but hardly plain in this case. An alternative title might have been 'The Big Bust Up'. It is a return to Bob's use of traditional melodies to hang his words on. On this occasion, it is 'Once I Had a Sweetheart', sometimes known as 'The Forsaken Lover'. There is also some evidence of it being derived from the old folk song 'I Once Loved a Lass', particularly with regard to the lyrics of the penultimate verse. As with many songs on this album, the guitar plays around the G, G6 and G7 chord shapes, with an occasional F thrown in for adornment.

This is a song that Bob later wished he had never recorded. It deals with the vitriolic final, great, screaming battle royal that took place at Suze's house and involved Bob, Suze and Carla (Suze's sister), an almighty row that finally put pay to their relationship: 'Beneath a bare light bulb the plaster did pound. Her sister and I in a screaming battleground.'

Bob doesn't hold back as he attacks Suze's sister (once his biggest fan and promoter), describing her in no uncertain terms as a parasite. Bob's fury came pouring out at Carla and Suze's mother (who we already know didn't approve of Bob). Yet ironically, in the end, it was Bob and his relationship with Joan Baez that had proved the final straw. He was to blame. Following her abortion, it was Suze who could no longer put up with the situation and ended it.

Although the song is centred on the great fight, it can also be construed as a heartfelt apology. Bob goes out of his way to put Suze on a pedestal and portrays her as an innocent vision of perfection, a goddess that he had foolishly, clumsily lost, and one that he cannot find a way to apologise to or forgive himself for what he has done.

He depicts himself as broken, the final verse summing up the misery of his life:

Ah, my friends from the prison, they ask unto me,
'How good, how good does it feel to be free?'
And I answer them most mysteriously
'Are birds free from the chains of the skyway?'

In a later interview, Suze was asked if she was hurt by the songs that Bob had written about their relationship and bust-up. She took a very conciliatory and understanding tone: 'It was the end of something and we both were hurt and bitter. His art was his outlet, his exorcism. It was healthy.'

'It Ain't Me Babe' (Bob Dylan)

The album concludes with one of Bob's most popular songs; a complete change of tone from the last song. Despite the beauty of the melody and power of the E, F and G chords, even the lamenting harmonica, this is dark and brutal. Bob's mood is angry and defiant. He is portraying his lover (Suze) as controlling and demanding. Now he is placing the blame for the breakdown of their relationship firmly on her. He is not to blame. She was trying to shackle him and he would not allow himself to be held in such a claustrophobic relationship. He needed his freedom. She should go away and leave him alone. He isn't what she's looking for.

Outtakes
There were nowhere near as many outtakes for this album. Bob's creativity was beginning to wane as a result of the pressure and life changes.

'Denise' (Bob Dylan)
This is basically a musical reworking of 'Black Crow Blues' played on the piano with a chugging bluesy harp and different lyrics. There is some humour in this, along with some clever lyrics, but the major feel of the piece is one of desolation. Who is this girl Denise? Is she for sale or just on the shelf? Is she after Bob? It's no good trying to throw him because he's already been tossed! This is Bob wallowing in the aftermath of the breakup.

'Mama You Been on My Mind' (Bob Dylan)
The melody on this is as strong and poignant as any that Bob has written. Using the C and rising G chords, he has created a song soaked and dripping with sorrow and yearning.

In the lyrics, Dylan puts on the pretence of indifference; for example, 'Where you been don't bother me nor bring me down with sorrow. I don't even mind who you'll be wakin' with tomorrow' may appear as if Bob is disinterested but suggests that, in reality, he is very much concerned about his lover. He's pacing the floors, bowed and bent, thinking of her all the time and eaten up with regret. He begs her not to be angry with him: 'I don't mean trouble, please don't put me down or get upset, I'm not pleadin' or sayin', I can't forget you.' But of course, he is pleading and saying he can't forget her.

The strength of the tune, with its unforgettable earworm of a melody, coupled with the superb flow of lyrics that drip out of the verses full of pathos and longing, make this one of Bob's top songs. It should feature up there with those similar triumphs such as 'It Ain't Me Babe,' and 'Don't Think Twice It's Alright', but he did not include it on the album. I can see why. The split with Suze was still raw.

Ironically, later, Joan Baez, smarting from her split with Bob, included a cover of this song 'Daddy You Been on My Mind' on her 1965 *Farewell Angelina* album. It was a song that was to be covered by a multitude of people – all of whom obviously recognised its incredible strengths.

'Mr Tambourine Man (with Ramblin' Jack Elliott)' (Bob Dylan)

There are shades of Easy Rider in the writing of this song. He began writing it on a road trip with friends to the New Orleans Mardi Gras in February 1964. One can only imagine the nature of that trip from the LSD-soaked Rimbaudian poetry. There was some confusion over where the song was finally completed. The Journalist Al Aronowitz claims he finished it while round at his house and Judy Collins says it was round at her place. He probably worked on it at both places!

He recorded it for the *Another Side of Bob Dylan* album with Ramblin' Jack Elliott singing harmony. However, the Ramblin' Jack vocals came out sounding a little flat and it was shelved. He recorded a demo for Witmark publishers and then recorded the track in a session six months later for the *Bringing it All Back Home* album.

'I'll Keep It With Mine' (Bob Dylan)

Bob really liked this track. He tried recording it a number of times over the course of three years. I'm not surprised; the melody is hypnotic and haunting, which is why he went back to it for *Bringing it All Home* and then again for *Blonde On Blonde*.

This piano version was recorded with the intention of including it on the album but was rejected. Bob knew that he could do better. The vocal and harmonica work fine, but the piano sounds too plodding to me.

The poetry of the lyrics is hard to interpret, but they appear to be another paean for Suze. The mysterious girl is looking for something but all the time it is there with him. He's waiting. He'll always be there.

For a time, Bob was dating Nico from The Velvet Underground and he gave her this song. She recorded it on her *Chelsea Girls* album. Her wistful breathy voice ideally suited the song.

Singles

Strangely, given the success of 'The Times They Are A-Changin'' plus the popularity and notoriety of Bob at this time, there were no singles released even though there were a number of tracks that would have been strong contenders and almost certainly would have been hits.

Bringing it All Back Home (1965)

Personnel:
Bob Dylan: acoustic guitar, piano, vocals and harmonica
Al Gorgoni: guitar
Kenny Rankin: guitar
Bruce Langhorne: guitar
John P. Hammond: guitar
Paul Griffin: piano, keyboards
Frank Owens: piano
Steve Boone: bass
Joseph Macho Jr: bass
John Sebastian: bass
William E. Lee: bass – 'It's All Over Now, Baby Blue'
Bobby Gregg: drummer
Danny Kramer: photography
Tom Wilson: producer
Label: Colombia
Recorded at Colombia Studio A
Release date: March 1965
Highest chart positions: UK: 1 US: 6

Bringing it All Back Home was another watershed album. Bob shed his skin to emerge from one assumed persona into a completely different one. Gone was the carefully honed Guthrie image with its rough and ready roustabout cool, in its place was the polka-dot shirt, tight pants and shades; the long-tousled hair and Brando-esque swagger of the New York hipster. Bob transformed himself into a Rock Star.

In many ways, this was not unexpected. Right from the start, he had been smitten with rock 'n' roll, particularly Little Richard. To an extent, the acoustic folk route had been a diversion, a means to earn a living, a vehicle to break through. Even on his first album, he had experimented with a band sound: his first single, 'Mixed Up Confusion' had been an electric number. The surprising thing was he had not ventured back into those electric experiments over the course of the next three albums.

There were a number of factors that sparked this sudden conversion. The first of these was meeting The Beatles and hitting it off so well with them. They were in awe of each other. The Beatles were knocked out by Dylan's poetic lyrics and content and Bob was bowled over by their musical dynamism, complex chord changes and intricate harmonies. At that first meeting, the hip Dylan had introduced the boys to marijuana and they had turned him back on to rock.

The second influence was that of John P. Hammond, a friend and son of John D. Hammond who had originally discovered, signed and produced Bob. John had gone electric and was giving his blues songs the treatment. Not only that, but he had used three members of The Hawks (later to go on to become The Band) in order to achieve this. Bob was impressed.

The third push came from The Byrds. They, too, had been fired up by The Beatles and had been moved to create a new style, marrying folk music to electric rock to create an early folk-rock style. They took Bob's 1964 'Mr Tambourine Man' and gave it the treatment with jangly twelve-string guitars. Not only was it a huge hit, but it caught Bob's imagination and drew him into a lifetime relationship with the band.

In 1965, Tom Wilson and Bob had experimented with overdubbing electric instruments onto some Dylan tracks. The results were deemed unsuccessful, though Tom went on to try the same thing with Simon and Garfunkel's 'Sound of Silence', which worked and created an enormous hit for them.

The seeds had been sown and when Bob went into the studio to record the next album, everything had changed. While the early sessions were acoustic, even the style and sound were radically different. The songs sounded more developed, smoother and more sophisticated. The poetry was still there, but the imagery was greatly different. There seemed a new anger in Bob and it was not directed in the same way. He seemed angry with everything. Bob was not highlighting social issues as he had done with his earlier songs – dubbed 'protest songs' by the media. Here he was hitting out at the establishment. The electric tracks were hard-hitting, vitriolic diatribes. A fury had been unleashed and this snarling new Dylan was growling like a pent-up panther.

There wasn't much about this new Dylan that appealed to his fanatical folk audience. The pop-star image looked like a sell-out. The electric sound was met with dismay. Folk music held an intellectual cache. It was music to be listened to, studied and discussed. Rock music was viewed as nothing short of trite, simplistic trivia. They found it difficult to take this new Dylan seriously. Rock and pop were juvenile; folk was intellectual.

The album was released in March and Bob's first outing with an electric band was in July at the Newport Folk Festival. He used Al Kooper on organ and the Paul Butterfield Blues band with Mike Bloomfield's searing lead. The reports differ as to the extent of the booing and the reasons. The speakers couldn't handle the overamplified sound, so the audience were not hearing the lyrics, but more importantly, they did not like this new rock version of Dylan. That was quite clear on Bob's 1966 electric world tour; the band was received with mixed reactions and a lot of booing and heckling. The shout of Judas at the Manchester concert clearly revealed the sentiments behind it. The more intellectual folkies saw electrification as a sell-out. They thought Dylan was going commercial and betraying them. Bob's reaction was to defiantly press on with what he wanted to do. His response to a heckler, followed by an instruction to the band, summed up his attitude: 'I don't believe you! You're a liar!' Turning to the band: 'Play fucking loud!'

This new electric Dylan was galvanised by the new music. He had been getting bored with his acoustic material and had even talked of giving up the business altogether. The complexities of working with a band, with a whole range of instruments, opened up new possibilities. He was fired up once again.

His success had brought new stresses and strains. A number of his old friends turned against this new Dylan. Bob saw it as jealousy. With a segment of the audience against him and a lot of his friends talking behind his back, he did not know who to trust.

Albert Grossman was doing what all managers do; he was guiding the career, milking the opportunities and looking to close deals. They had signed up to produce a book; there were concert tours and record deals, media conferences, TV and radio. Bob was touring with a typewriter, trying to tap out chapters of *Tarantula* in dressing rooms, writing new songs to keep up with demand and undertaking the gruelling round of airports, trains, hotel rooms and gigs. The fans were everywhere demanding a piece of him. The media swamped him. Then there was his entourage of friends, hangers-on and management. He was in the circus. The only way of coping was to medicate with drugs. Amphetamines to keep the energy. Downers to turn off. Marijuana for pleasure and nicotine from habit. Then there was LSD and even mention of heroin. He was a young man out for a good time, burning that candle at both ends and in the middle.

The documentary film *Don't Look Back* was a black-and-white record of the 1965 tour of the UK shot with a handheld sixteen-millimetre camera by D. A. Pennebaker, who had been commissioned by Bob and his management. It is a classic 'fly on the wall' documentary, which formed a template for all future rockumentaries, that clearly showed the incredible pressures that Bob was under at the time – endless partying with rock cognoscenti, interviews, entertaining, travelling, meeting fans, performing. Bob never had room to be himself, never could relax. It seemed incredible that in the midst of this endless chaos, he was trying to write his book and new songs. When Bob saw the final version he was unhappy with it, saying that it did not provide the full picture and needed re-editing. Later he relented and allowed it out as it was.

Bob's muses had changed too. He added the Beat poets to his inspiration. Allen Ginsberg had come into the picture. You can see him in the alley on the promo of 'Subterranean Homesick Blues'. The Beat poetry added an urban cutting edge to the Rimbaudian imagery. He was adding the boosters to his poetry. With the psychedelic experiences adding a fifth dimension, we were heading for the stratosphere.

This new Dylan was wired, hip, sharp and acerbic. He came over as twitchy, nervy and angry – a wary defensive tiger looking ready to pounce. The world was out to get him. With his small entourage of equally cocky, hip friends, they would enjoy tearing apart anyone who penetrated their bubble. The put-downs and eviscerations could be cruel.

The album cover for *Bringing it All Home* was taken by Daniel Kramer round at Albert Grossman's house. An intense, almost scowling, Dylan is peering out. He may be cradling a kitten, but those fists are clenched in a pugilistic pose. He's wearing a smart, tailored shirt with cuff links and a black jacket. His hair is a little longer and Daniel has him in a halo created by an attachment to the camera lens – but he's no angel. Albert Grossman's wife Sally is lounging in the background, carefully posed in her red trouser suit, with a casual cigarette. Bob has a magazine open and has carefully arranged albums and paraphernalia. *Another Side of Bob Dylan* is poking out from behind Sally. There are albums by The Impressions, Robert Johnson, Ravi Shankar, Eric Von Schmidt and Lotte Lenya (singing Brecht). Woody is noticeably absent. There is *Time Magazine* and a fallout shelter sign – covers are important.

The back cover notes are written by Bob in a stream of consciousness that could have come straight out of *Tarantula* and probably did. His latest work of art is to write 'WHAAAT?' on his favourite wall.

'Subterranean Homesick Blues' (Bob Dylan)

Dylan doesn't ease us in gently with one of the acoustic offerings from the album. We're straight in the deep end. You don't need much telling to know this is going to be different. The opening track is an explosion of incandescent rage discharging in a vitriolic description of the system that controls us. Inspired by Chuck Berry's 'Too Much Monkey Business', the searing guitar riff and machine gun bullet words splatter their aural dynamite in a stream of invective.

This is not so much social comment but rather a rant of random observations concerning the society we live in:

Look out kid
You're gonna get hit
By losers, cheaters
Six-time users
Hangin' 'round the theatres
Girl by the whirlpool
Lookin' for a new fool
Don't follow leaders
Watch the parkin' meters

This is Dylan at the heart of the new counterculture, hip to what's going down, advocating dropping out of this rat race of a system. There's the drug culture with Johnny mixing up the medicine, the social division between conservative, straight culture and the new burgeoning youth culture with its rejection of the establishment and opposition to 'their' war in Vietnam. The kids instantly recognised the message and could identify with it. The dense lyrics contained images of undercover narcs, backhanders, phoney religion, inequality and the constant harrying by the establishment. He was describing their world. If you didn't dress right, talk right and act right you couldn't get on. You had to fit in. Bob's answer was to drop out, go underground and take away the handle so the pump no longer worked. Bob was siding with the kids against the state – 180 degrees from his later stance following the motorbike accident, where he distanced himself from the counterculture and repudiated all it stood for.

The name of the song reveals the Beat poetry that fuelled it, emanating straight from a minor novel by Jack Kerouac called *The Subterraneans*. The lyrics had more in common with Allen Ginsberg's *Howl* than they did with anything Arthur Rimbaud had written.

Musically this is out-and-out rock with a heavy country-tinged backbeat, busy instrumentation that melds into a sound that makes it difficult to separate the instruments and bursts of harmonica between the verses. The electric guitar chimes and pierces the entire piece. Dylan's vocal is clear and distinct. The overall result is a completely new sound – not as brutal a sound as we later hear at Newport, a tad muddier and more complex, but just as powerful. As for the lyrics – they look as if Bob has used the Pete Seeger song 'Taking it Easy' as the Launchpad for his barbed poetry.

The song was released as a single and the promo video was every bit as innovative, heralded as the first artistic promo video. It features a cool straight-faced Dylan holding a set of cue cards with keywords from the song printed on them, dropping them one after the other as the song progresses. Very effective. Allen Ginsberg and Bob Neuwirth look on before walking off at the song's conclusion whilst Bob dusts his hands. Whoa! This snarling epic is confronting the beast head-on. It's relentless.

'She Belongs to Me' (Bob Dylan)

Bob lowers the tempo and changes the mood for this second number. So who is this fabled woman? Bob says she belongs to him, yet she is nobody's. He puts her on a pedestal. She's a goddess, a queen, a pagan spirit who requires worship and allegiance. She's an artist who can do anything. You'll do anything for her. Then she'll reduce you to a subservient voyeur. The consensus is that the muse is Joan Baez, though others think it might be Dylan harking back to Suze or even proposing that it is Nico. Then again, the enigmatic Sara Lowndes was on the scene. Some think it's a metaphor for America.

Although it is a blues arrangement in the key of A major, with a capo on the second fret, and revolves around the chords of G, C and A, it is far from a blues. It's far too smooth and jazzy. There is a full band on here, with Bruce Langhorn's guitar much to the fore, but they produce a light, almost acoustic feel over which Bob can sing his poetry in a relaxed manner. The result is a delightful laid-back vibe that is light and airy and shows off the poetry to good effect.

'Maggie's Farm' (Bob Dylan)

After the poetic interlude, we're straight back into a blistering rock track. This too, follows a standard blues structure with repeated lines – Bob and the band let rip.

Another anthem of the counterculture – Maggie's Farm being the establishment – or is this just Dylan rebelling about the workload and stress that's been loaded on his back? I don't think so. Bob rails about exploitation, abuse and control. He's got a head full of ideas and he's made to do menial tasks. He insinuates that the establishment lies about everything. He finishes by griping about the pressure to conform: 'Well, I try my best to be just like I am, but everybody wants you to be just like them. They say 'sing while you slave', and I just get bored.' At this moment in time, Bob was clearly identifying with the youth rebellion. He had embraced beat culture and you didn't get more anti-establishment than that.

Even though musically it's quite basic, an electric blues played in the key of G major and working largely around variations of the E chord, the way the guys play it with such gusto and flair transforms it into something more. When performed at Newport with Mike Bloomfield ripping it with his searing jagged lead guitar, they unleashed a monster. This studio version was not as ragged or raw but still powerful enough to raise hairs on the neck.

'Love Minus Zero/No Limit' (Bob Dylan)

After the acerbic torrent of 'Maggie's Farm', we are taken drifting on the lilting silky winds of a balmy love song. While this is another electric number, the tone is soft, gentle and soothing. Dylan's guitar is in a drop C tuning. The capo on the fourth fret creates the key of E major. The chords of C, D, F and G are deployed to create a hook of descending chords.

Dylan talks of 'my love' as if this is a particular woman, but it could also be a generalised female muse or his own intrinsic love. In my mind, he is referring to Joan Baez, who is an artist and to whom he once gave an Egyptian ring. But it could be Suze Rotollo (who is also an artist), Sara or Nico. This love he refers to is absolute, elemental and pure.

The verses follow a pattern with the lines in rhymes or half rhymes. The first four lines of the stanza concern society, while the last two lines reveal his love's calm reaction to it.

The commerce of everyday life, with all its social interactions, carries on, but his love remains serene, all-knowing, transcending the mundane. People recite without understanding, but his love understands it all and remains aloof. His love requires no frippery or showy displays. She's above that. She knows that money and possessions cannot bring understanding.

Towards the end, the poem becomes darker as death and illness lurk. Then things become twisted around in the last verse – this all-knowing, zen-like powerful woman is also vulnerable and damaged, requiring comfort, succour and healing.

Above: Hip rock star Dylan in 1965 wearing a psychedelic shirt. *(Alamy)*

Left: First album *Bob Dylan* released in 1962, featuring a fresh-faced 21-year-old Dylan in sheepskin coat and corduroy Woody Guthrie cap. *(Columbia)*

Right: 1963's *Freewheelin'* album – photo by Don Hunstein. A hunched-up Bob with Suze Rotolo huddling on a freezing New York day on Jones Street. *(Columbia)*

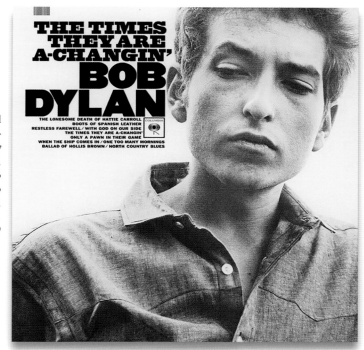

Right: Third album 1964 – *The Times They Are a-Changin'*, featuring a photo of a young Bob Dylan still in thrall to Woody Guthrie. *(Columbia)*

Left: Fourth album 1964 – *Another Side of Bob Dylan* with Bob changing into a different style of songwriting. *(Columbia)*

Left: Bob on WBC TV for the first time in 1963 performing 'Blowin' in the Wind' in his Guthrie-style working clothes.

Right: A close-up of Bob with his wire harmonica rack performing 'Blowin' in the Wind'.

Left: Bob performing 'North Country Blues' at the Newport Folk Festival in 1963.

Right: Bob at Newport 1963 with an admiring Judy Collins looking on and Doc Watson to his right.

Left: Bob and Joan Baez performing 'It Ain't Me Babe' at the Newport Folk Festival in 1964.

Right: Close-up of the King and Queen of folk performing 'It Ain't Me Babe' at the Newport Folk Festival in 1964.

Left: The iconic 1965 *Bringing it All Back Home* cover. The rock Dylan goes electric as a reclining Sally Grossman looks on. *(Columbia)*

Right: Rock star Dylan poses in a Triumph T-shirt with Bob Neuwirth holding a camera behind in this 1965 *Highway 61* cover. *(Columbia)*

Right: The soft-focussed, tousle-haired, strung-out Dylan posing for the 1966 cover of *Blonde on Blonde*. *(Columbia)*

Left: The 1967 *John Wesley Harding* cover, featuring a countrified Dylan with two Bengali Bauls and a carpenter. *(Columbia)*

Left: Newport 1964 with Pete Seeger in the background – before the divisive electric onslaught of 1965.

Right: The music video for 'Subterranean Homesick Blues' with Beat poet Allen Ginsberg to the left.

Left: A new cool Dylan peels away cards with lyrics on in what is, perhaps, the first rock promo video.

Right: Dylan goes electric! Dylan played the Newport Festival in 1965 with Barry Goldberg and Al Cooper and, from the Paul Butterfield Blues Band, guitarist Mike Bloomfield, bassist Jerome Arnold and drummer Sam Lay.

Left: On the plane for the notorious England Tour of 1965.

Right: Bob being interviewed in a hotel room with the typewriter he was writing *Tarantula* on during the England Tour of 1965.

Left: Rock star, electric Dylan fronting The Hawks on his controversial 1966 World Tour.

Right: A casually dressed Dylan in shades in a hotel on his World Tour 1966.

Left: On stage performing with an electric guitar on the World Tour 1966.

Right: Blurry close-up with sharp mic from the Manchester Trade Hall 'Judas' concert in 1966.

Left: A 1969 clean-cut, cleaned-up Bob performing 'Girl From the North Country' with Johnny Cash on *The Johnny Cash Show*.

Right: A relaxed, countrified Bob performing 'Girl From the North Country' with Johnny Cash on *The Johnny Cash Show*.

Left: The cover of 1969's *Nashville Skyline*, featuring relaxed, country Dylan with hat and acoustic guitar. *(Columbia)*

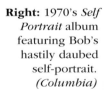

Right: 1970's *Self Portrait* album featuring Bob's hastily daubed self-portrait. *(Columbia)*

Right: 1970's *New Morning* album showcasing a pensive Dylan with fluffy beard and sepia tones. *(Columbia)*

Left: The triple album *Biograph* retrospective. *(Columbia)*

Left: The fabulous *Bootleg Series Vol 1-3*, featuring a wealth of unreleased material from 1961 onwards. *(Columbia)*

Right: The magnificent 1966 double-disc electric live show from the Manchester Trade Hall, featuring the 'Judas' incident. *(Columbia/Legacy)*

Left: The soundtrack to the Martin Scorsese documentary of Dylan 1961-1966. The cover was shot at the Aust Ferry Terminal in 1966. *(Columbia/Legacy)*

Right: A young Bob in 1964 tapping away on his typewriter, producing song lyrics for the Witmark Publishing house. *(Columbia/ Legacy)*

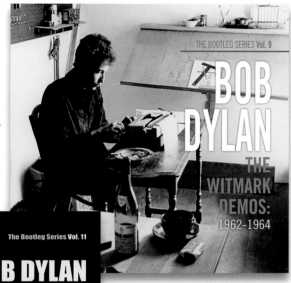

Left: The 1967 recording with The Band in the basement at Big Pink in Woodstock. *(Columbia/ Legacy)*

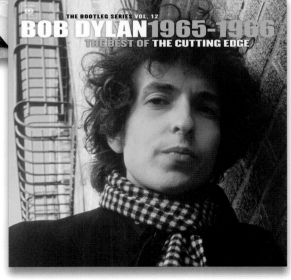

Right: The outtakes and alternative tracks from the three mid-sixties electric albums. *(Columbia/Legacy)*

Above: The 1970 new image Dylan in the backyard at Woodstock. *(Elliot Landy)*

For me, the nihilistic line 'No success like failure and failure is no success at all' really stands out. It says to me that all life is ultimately pointless, but we do it anyway, continue to strive, and live our lives in the moment.

'Outlaw Blues' (Bob Dylan)

After the gentle sophistication of the last track, we're straight into a raw blues riff played on a rhythm guitar around the chords E and A. The guitar is dirty, visceral and repetitive. Bob's voice is to the fore with the overdubbed harmonica, a lead guitar sprinkling notes, and the rest of the band adorning the background.

This is a typical blues, with Bob repeating the lines over the basic riff. All very standard for a blues but nonetheless very compelling. That riff eats into you. Then we have Bob's words, inspired by Odetta's 'I'm A Stranger Here' – but this is no common or garden blues. The words are surreal and oblique, with humorous images, but the message is clear. Bob sees himself as a fugitive on the run. He's fleeing through the swamp with the hounds on his trail, an outlaw like Jesse James. Robert Ford was a member of the Jesse James gang who made a deal with the governor to avoid being hanged and shot Jesse in the back. Bob has no home and wishes he could escape to some far-off place – get away from it all. He's wearing his disguise and needs all the luck he can get. He's fed up with this rat race and being asked all these stupid questions: 'Don't ask me nothin' about nothin', I just might tell you the truth.'

The last verse feels strange, an add-on. The reference to a brown skin woman – but he loves her just the same – sounds odd. It doesn't sit easily with today's sensibilities, even if it was an attempt to promote some kind of equality. It sounds clumsy. Is he looking for refuge with some lover? Why the racial reference? Is it to do with the civil rights SNCC?

The track was recorded as an acoustic version the day before.

'On the Road Again' (Bob Dylan)

The song starts with a wailing harmonica, then the band pitch in with a chugging twelve-bar blues based around chords A, D and E. Behind this steady rhythm, a lead guitar can be heard picking a chiming slew of notes, again, back in the mix. The track drives along with the harmonica accentuating the verses.

The title is double-edged. On the one hand, we have the reference to 'On the Road', the classic beat novel by Jack Kerouac – the king of the beats, who Bob was greatly influenced by – on the other, we have the blues song 'On the Road' by the Memphis Jug Band. Things are rarely simple or straightforward with Bob.

On the surface, this is a comic song, but there are many levels of interpretation, as Bob used to enjoy writing and performing during this period. The circus is in town and we're in it. Here he is – the creative poet/ musician up against the establishment. He is living in an insane society where nothing makes any sense. It's all just a mad game. The ridiculousness of the world is exemplified by the absurd behaviour of his in-laws. But then it could be cataloguing the equally crazy goings on in bohemia.

'Bob Dylan's 115th Dream' (Bob Dylan)

One satirical comic offering follows another in this sequel to the 1963 'Dream'. Here Bob amalgamates two seminal American elements – *Moby Dick* and the hunt for the mythical white whale, and the Mayflower and Columbus's discovery of America. In this surreal dream, with all its bizarre episodes, Bob lampoons the whole of American culture in an oblique set of mad escapades – from the immorality of buying the place with beads to the culture of building forts and waging war.

The surreal story is both absurd and hilarious and thunders along at a grand pace. The fun of the piece is exemplified by the hilarity at the beginning. Bob starts off with his acoustic and the band fails to come in. He breaks down into helpless laughter. On the second start, the band then enter with the characteristic sound they had crafted for this album. The rhythm section sets up a good pace, the chiming lead bubbles along and it all gels together wonderfully. The actual music has been used before and is an electrified 'Motorcycle Nightmare'.

To say the tale is weird is an understatement. It verges on slapstick. The hobo sailor with Captain Arab and his crew (a play on Ahab from Moby Dick) discover 'modern' America and lay claim to it. The first thing they do is take a big breath and faint due to the pollution. After getting arrested for carrying harpoons, the tale gets increasingly bizarre as Bob tries to get a meal by impersonating a food critic, attempts to get money from a bank to bail his friends out and exposes himself as collateral, seeks help from a funeral parlour advertising brotherhood and deals with the hard right patriot who threatens to kill him, getting robbed in the alley. It's a land where religion receives lip service, everywhere is greed, selfishness and exploitation. Everyone is after a buck. Bureaucracy rules. Nobody wants to help. The images are wonderful – bowling balls, a foot through the telephone, in and out the other door of a cab, an Englishman says Fab.

Towards the end of this hilarious, fantastic expose of modern society, he decides to bail out, takes the parking ticket off the mast and sails off. He spies three ships. The Captain says he is Columbus. Bob says, 'Good luck.'

'Mr Tambourine Man' (Bob Dylan)

Side two starts with a more acoustic vibe. Dylan's acoustic, with its drop D tuning and capo on the third fret sounds bright and cheery. The melody played out in the chord shapes G, A and D sound joyous and sparkly, creating an uplifting start to the side. The only accompaniment is a superlative light, sympathetic lead guitar from Bruce Langhorne. Bob sings it gaily with rousing harmonica.

Mr Tambourine Man was composed in 1964 on the same drug-fuelled Mardi Gras trip to New Orleans that had produced 'The Chimes of Freedom'. Indeed, it has the same feel to it as 'Chimes'. It probably would have appeared on *Another Side of Bob Dylan* if the recording with Jack Elliott had worked out. This was prior to him veering off into the more Beat-orientated poetry and was much more informed by Arthur Rimbaud in terms of its expansive imagery – if one can conceive of Rimbaud soaked in acid.

The surreal lyrics, with their Rimbaudian imagery and rhymes, sweep you along into a joyous search. Despite Bob's assertions to the contrary, the lyrics seem to be based around an LSD trip. Bob, having stayed up all night, weary but ecstatically euphoric, follows his muse through landscapes and experience, immersing him in the glorious textures of inspiration. Dawn finds him wandering through the empty streets, as melodies and poems swirl around him, waiting to be grasped. His delirious happiness is boundless as he reaches for the tunes to hang his words on. Far from the circus of society, he desires to be free in the wonders of nature, on the beach of infinity, to put everything aside and bask in the moment, consumed by the wonder of creation that his muse is presenting him with.

A mind worm of a song that inspired so many. The Byrds' version, recorded from a 1964 demo, was not only instrumental in creating folk rock, propelling them into the charts, but also gave Bob that extra boost to going electric and producing this album. The circle was complete.

Amazingly this track was recorded in the same session that produced 'Gates of Eden', 'It's All Over Now Baby Blue' and 'It's Alright Ma (I'm Only Bleeding)' – one giant of a recording session that would be hard to equal anywhere.

'Gates of Eden' (Bob Dylan)

The acoustic style continues on side two with this lengthy masterpiece featuring just Bob, his acoustic and harmonica. Amazingly, despite the complexity of its chord sequences, changing from G, D, F, C and B, and the density of the bizarre lyric with its literary and biblical references, the song was recorded in one single take in the same session that produced half the album.

The piece, composed in 1964 shortly after 'Chimes' and 'Tambourine', is dour, verging on the depressing, as it describes in convoluted, covert poetic elaborations, the decaying rudiments of a vacuous society where even the erudite and wise are objects of ridicule from within Eden. Everyone is on a journey to achieve their own paradise, but it remains beyond their grasp, all is phoney, all is a game played out in a mindless world. All the possessions, exploits and knowledge count for nothing in Eden – power and image are of no consequence. Even reality, jealousy and judgement are pointless. There are no saviours. Truth is beyond us. Death is all that is real, with shades of Blake and Milton's *Paradise Lost*.

'It's Alright Ma (I'm Only Bleeding)' (Bob Dylan)

For me, this song is the apotheosis of, not only this album, but the whole of Dylan's canon. The poetry is a vicious diatribe against the hypocrisy and lunacy of human culture epitomised by the world Bob finds himself in and the United States in particular. He analyses it and tears it to bits. But it's okay, he is not going to allow it to destroy him. The music is every bit as strident and angry as the lyrics. The acoustic guitar has real edge and bite. It's in drop D tuning with a capo on the second fret and played in the key of E minor, which gives it a sharp sound. Although the chord progression based around G, D, and A is similar to that used by the Everly Brothers on 'Wake Up Little Suzie', the way Bob hits those strings strikes a strident anger.

Bob may have stopped finger-pointing at specific people or overtly supporting causes such as civil rights and the anti-war movement, but that had not prevented him from venting his fury at the establishment. In this song, he lets fly at every aspect of modern society, from the hypocrisy of religion, those who create the rules, those who judge, those who claim to have answers to life, the consumers, commercialism, those who brainwash and advertise, those who use anger, fear and violence, those who create this straitjacket of claustrophobic shallowness to those who would try to pull you down. Every aspect of our stultifying culture is exposed and found wanting.

Rarely has a song contained such scope and venom. The mess created by corporate America, with its control, lies and propaganda, is laid bare. The anger Bob feels is extant, as is his determination to not allow it to cloud his judgement or take away his freedom. He is above the pettiness: 'And if my thought dreams could be seen, they'd probably put my head in a guillotine. But it's alright, Ma, it's life, and life only.'

'It's All Over Now, Baby Blue' (Bob Dylan)

The side finishes with another acoustic offering. Bob's acoustic guitar and harmonica are augmented by William E. Lee's bass guitar. The result is as powerful as if it was fully electric. This time the guitar is tuned to drop C with a capo on the fourth fret. The chords C, G, F, D and E create a moving melody for this sad song. The mournful harmonica enhances Bob's soulful delivery. It's all over now. Get out. Everything has changed. It's time to move on.

Although the song is usually associated with the breakup with Joan Baez, as with many of Bob's songs, the inspiration is probably more complicated than that. 'Baby Blue' is probably a composite. Sections of the lyrics may be directed at a particular person, while others either at someone else or a whole group of people. At the time, Bob was moving away from his acoustic folk roots and hitting a lot of friction on the way. A number of his friends had turned against him and there was a lot of backbiting surrounding him going electric. In typical Dylan fashion, he brushed this off and refused to compromise: 'Leave your stepping stones behind, something calls for you. Forget the dead you've left; they will not follow you.'

As a breakup song to a lover, it is extremely harsh. The sentiments are quite callous and cruel though the beautiful melody disguises the severity of the message.

That is it. Bob's first electric album (even if one side is largely acoustic). Completely groundbreaking – from the various unique sounds the band created to the surreal symbolism and Beat poetry. This was a new Dylan.

Outtakes:
'California' (Bob Dylan)
One of Bob's blues riff piano pieces. The track sounds more like an impromptu solo run-through in the studio than a proper take. Bob is pounding the piano, stamping his foot in time and giving the odd blast of harmonica. It's a classic blues with repeated lines. If developed, it would have been as good as any of Bob's similar bluesy piano numbers. In the event, the last verse was used in the 'Outlaw Blues' number that he recorded in the same session. That track superseded 'California' and put an end to it being worked on any further. In fact, that last verse makes more sense in the context of the 'California' track – in terms of the dark sunglasses.

'Farewell Angelina' (Bob Dylan)
Undoubtedly one of Bob's more important songs to have evaded a proper recording. With its obscure, dreamlike lyrics flowing in true Rimbaudian symbolism, it is open to much interpretation.

Bob only attempted to record this song once, which is strange as it possesses a haunting melody, is poetically complex, and would have sat nicely on *Bringing it All Back Home*. The melody is taken from a traditional song that was sung by Pete Seeger called 'Wagoner's Lad'. Bob had already used the melody on another song that never saw the light of day – 'I Rode Out One Morning'.

The drop C tuning with the capo on the seventh fret gives the guitar a light chiming quality, being so high up on the fretboard, that is at odds with the vocal. Bob sings it in a dour dirge – probably why he did not include it on the album. The Joan Baez version is much brighter and fully brings out the melody. Maybe Bob could hear what was wrong but couldn't see the way of brightening it up so never attempted it again?

The song is undoubtedly about the break-up between Bob and Joan Baez. Bob is suggesting that the good times are over and there are battles to be fought elsewhere. He has to go. They have loved deeply and there is no fault. I interpret these lines as a description of what has happened:

The jack and the queen
Have forsake the courtyard
Fifty-two gypsies

Now file past the guards
In the space where the deuce
And the ace once ran wild

They were the Jack and the Queen of Folk (Bob's being gracious) but
have both moved on. There's a new game in town. The cards are open to
inspection, anything can happen. She was the sovereign ace and he was the
lowly vagabond deuce and they had a great time. No regrets. They have to
leave the sycophants, managers, hangers-on and minions behind. The circus
is moving on. It is a sentimental song of great empathetic tenderness.

Bob later spoke of Joan in affectionate terms but with a touch of hardness.
He recognised what she had done for him but could also see what he had
done for her. The slate was even: 'She brought me up. I rode on her, but I
don't think I owe her anything.'

'If You Gotta Go, Go Now (Or Else You Got to Stay All Night)'
(Bob Dylan)
The band version, recorded in the *Bringing it All Back Home* sessions, was
preceded by a couple of acoustic recordings.

A fun upbeat number deploying the chords G and D7 that deals with the
sexual politics of the time. The band gives it the full treatment and sounds
more than a little influenced by the scouse fab four. It surges along with
a great pop sensibility based around a solid beat. The lead guitar bubbles
along with tinkling piano and some characteristic harmonica as Bob delivers
the lyrics with mischievous intent. He was renowned around the village as a
womanising ladies' man and this humorous offering captured the bohemian
mood of the times.

Having said that, these were still conservative days when sex was a
complete taboo. The sexual revolution was only just taking off in the general
society, even if it was pretty open in the culture Bob had been immersed in.
Even as late as 1967, the Stones were hitting trouble with their single 'Let's
Spend the Night Together', so this was pretty adventurous.

The song was covered by numerous bands. Manfred Mann had a sizeable
hit with it and Fairport Convention did a great French version. Despite it
being easy on the ear, it was not considered suitable for the album.

'I'll Keep it With Mine' (Bob Dylan)
This song had been knocking about since 1964 when Bob laid down a demo
for Witmark. He attempted a piano version during the *Bringing it All Back
Home* sessions but wasn't happy with the results. He attempted it once more
with a full band, under the title 'Bank Account Blues', for the *Blonde on
Blonde* album but still wasn't happy with that either.

The piano version is a wistful number, simply played, with a great melody
and Bob delivers it in his most plaintive vocal. It is a great love song in which

he remonstrates with his girl. She's leaving him in search of love. He's telling her that she's already found what she's looking for.

The song has been covered by multiple people, but in 1967 he offered it to Nico, with whom he was romantically attached. She produced the definitive version in her heavily accented breathy voice.

'You Don't Have to Do That' (Bob Dylan)
Little more than an interesting fragment with a simple G – C figure, sounding as if it might well be influenced by the Beatles. As we only have the first verse, it's not really possible to see where it's going. Bob's girl is leaving and he's telling her she doesn't have to do that. It would have been interesting to see how this might have developed had Bob taken it further. It had potential.

'Love is Just a Four Letter Word' (Bob Dylan)
This one can't really be called an outtake, as Bob never attempted to record it. He was writing it while on tour in 1965. In the documentary *Don't Look Back*, Joan Baez sings a verse of it and tells Bob that she'll record it herself if he finishes it. Joan Baez did just that and made a great job delivering Bob's wistful melody and lyrics.

It is a sad song full of nostalgia for a past love and an overheard conversation. The young Dylan viewed love as a trap but, with the wisdom of experience, came to realise that it was so much more.

Singles
'Maggie's Farm' b/w 'On The Road Again'
Strangely, given the success of 'The Times They Are A-Changin'' in the UK charts, this follow-up single did nothing in the US and only reached 22 in the Top 30 in the UK.

'Subterranean Homesick Blues' b/w 'She Belongs to Me'
'Subterranean Homesick Blues' was a commercial breakthrough for Dylan. It was the first single to get into the US *Billboard* Top 50 and returned Bob back to the Top Ten in the UK. Going electric had not put a halt to Bob's commercial popularity, far from it.

Highway 61 Revisited (1965)

Personnel:
Bob Johnson: producer
Tom Wilson: producer on 'Like a Rolling Stone'
Bob Dylan: guitar, piano, vocals acme siren and harmonica
Mike Bloomfield: electric guitar
Charlie McCoy: guitar on 'Desolation Row'
Al Kooper: organ, piano
Paul Griffin: organ, piano
Frank Owens: piano
Harvey Brooks: bass
Russ Savakus: bass guitar and upright bass on 'Desolation Row'
Joe Macho Jr: bass on 'Like a Rolling Stone'
Bobby Gregg: drums
Sam Lay: drums on 'Highway 61 Revisited'
Bruce Langhorne: tambourine
Daniel Kramer: photography
Don Hunstein: photography
Label: Colombia
Recorded at Colombia Studio A
Release date: August 1965
Highest chart positions: UK: 4 US: 3

Highway 61 Revisited picked up where *Bringing it All Back Home* left off. Despite the furore over the electrification, *Bringing it All Back Home* and its singles had proved commercially successful. They had sold better and reached higher in the charts than any of the previous material. But then, that only seemed to reinforce the protests and vindicate their view that he was selling out. The album was revolutionary in the way it took the blues-based music to other places, built on it, merging it with his surreal dystopian poetry outlining the corruption and collapse of American society. Bob continued to use Mike Bloomfield in the studio to provide that hard steely blues edge that he wanted. Apart from one track, this was to be a complete electric album.

By this time, relationships with his friends and contemporaries in the Greenwich Village folk community had become very strained and fractious. The pressures on Bob were beginning to show. The 'new' Dylan appeared arrogant and distant with a snarling, vitriolic set of put-downs. Many people felt the full extent of his barbed wit as he hit out at those rivals who dared to question his direction. Most notable was falling out with Phil Ochs, who had dared to criticise his single 'Won't You Please Crawl Out the Window' and suggested it wasn't as good as the previous. Dylan, without the guiding hand of Suze or the support of Joan Baez, was feeling very isolated and got at. He had surrounded himself with a sycophantic entourage and developed a siege mentality. The drugs were not helping. Amphetamine was giving him the energy to get through the gruelling workload but was making him twitchy and short-tempered.

The animosity emanating from the backbiting and two-faced relationships of his past friends came to the fore on a number of the songs, most notably on the vitriolic single 'Positively Fourth Street'. This was the snarling hip Dylan so adept at tearing reporters and unwanted guests to shreds with his quick-fire sarcasm.

Highway 61 Revisited was an interesting title. Hibbing is a small mining town of some 16,000 people in Minnesota up in the Midwest. Dylan grew up there in a tight-knit Jewish family that he found quite claustrophobic. The nearest big town was Duluth, on the shore of Lake Superior. Highway 61 was a major highway that ran some 1,400 miles all the way down from Duluth to New Orleans in the Deep South. New Orleans was a melting pot of blues, cajun, r&b, rock 'n' roll, country 'n' western and rockabilly. For a boy steeped in music, that road represented all that was great in the world. That road was the Shangri-La of musical heaven. It connected him to what he craved:

> Highway 61, the main thoroughfare of the country blues, begins about where I began. I always felt like I'd started on it, always had been on it and could go anywhere, even down into the deep Delta country. It was the same road, full of the same contradictions, the same one-horse towns, the same spiritual ancestors... It was my place in the universe, always felt like it was in my blood.

Now, as a successful musician, Bob was reconnecting with that dream.

On the front cover, a surly-looking Dylan, dressed in a bright shirt, motorcycle T-shirt and blue trousers, stares out. Behind him, we see the legs of a man with a camera dangling from his hand. There's no sign of the Guthrie vagabond; this is Dylan the confident James Dean rock star. He's taking no prisoners. It's a challenging stare. The cherubic face is still there, but this is a much more uncompromising Dylan.

The back cover notes are another bizarre stream of consciousness straight out of the writing he was doing for *Tarantula*. It did not have to make sense – merely convey the vibe.

We were set for the second electric masterpiece from this new persona – the switched-on hip-rock giant. This incarnation was steeped in Beat poetry. The French symbolism was taking a back seat. The finger-pointing was gone. What we had here was an angry Dylan raging against the establishment and identifying strongly with the outsiders and misfits. This was a Dylan with a vision. He was at home with his new band and knew exactly what sound he wanted to create. Bob was taking the blues and taking it somewhere else, somewhere new. He knew what he wanted. He was after that thin, wild mercury sound that would coalesce on the next album. But for me, this was the pinnacle. I was blown away by its hard edge and uncompromising style. He was heading out down that highway and blasting everything out of his way.

'Like a Rolling Stone' (Bob Dylan)
Many people think that this is Bob's perfect masterpiece.

After returning disillusioned from his UK tour, fed up with his songs and ready to quit, he wrote twenty pages of 'vomit' in which he let it all hang out. Playing about on the piano, he came up with the phrase 'how does it feel', which brought it all together. He condensed the words into a series of verses.

The lyrics illustrate the inequality in society by addressing the fall from grace of someone who has lived the high life, where everything is taken for granted, and now finds herself in the gutter, scrabbling around on the streets. She rudely finds that life for ordinary people is hard and based on compromise. Previous to that, it had all been so easy. She had allowed other people to perform for her: 'You shouldn't let other people get your kicks for you.' But this was real life, without any safety net. You sold what you had to: 'When you got nothing, you got nothing to lose.'

The song was thought to have come out of Bob's experience with Andy Warhol, Edie Sedgewick being the person in question. Though, like all of Bob's songs, it is probably much more complex than that.

The music came together through a gruelling 34 takes. This was incredibly unusual for Bob as he was used to either doing tracks in one take or schooling the band through a few takes. It demonstrates how important this was. Bob wanted to get it right. This track was a renewal; an attempt at creating a new sound. This was the template for what was to come. It was important to get it as near perfect as he could. Listening to the evolution via the recordings of the various takes, one can hear how it moves from a bluesy riff into something more complex and original. It was the introduction of Al Kooper's organ that transformed it.

This new sound was transformational. Based on a solid swaying rhythm section, with a subdued lead that occasionally bursts through, the song is consolidated by the organ that drives it into a momentous conflagration, a fusion of sound, that is quite different to anything that has preceded it. The search for this sound was something that had revived Bob and brought him back from the dead. Suddenly he was energised. He had something to believe in and work towards. This reinvigoration set Bob up for the next assault. It generated a new burst of creative energy.

'Tombstone Blues' (Bob Dylan)
An energised blues number that charges off at a slick pace in the key of F major. A hammer blow of percussion bangs out the pulse and sets up a solid base for the drum and bass to build on. The rhythm guitar slashes out the basic riff based on E and A chords over which everything is laid. The organ is used to fatten up the sound and Mike Bloomfield's lead guitar breaks into

searing runs not dissimilar to those deployed at Newport. The result is an energised romp, careering, threatening to fly off the track and whirls Bob's lyrics into a tornado of vitriol.

Using a slew of historical and biblical characters deployed in a lysergic-tinged dream sequence of bizarre scenes, Bob makes scathing attacks on the establishment, the abuse of power and the hypocrisy of organised religion. He has the vicious murderer Jack the Ripper in charge of the Chamber of Commerce. He has the prophet John the Baptist torturing a thief, sickened by what he has done and reporting to his commander in chief (God? Jesus?), who replies: 'death to all those who would whimper and die'. He has those in authority sending out soldiers to die, making insincere gestures of sorrow at their deaths and locking up any leaders who might threaten his position. The soldiers are burning villages and the TV preachers are craving fame. Musical geniuses such as Ma Rainey and Beethoven have been superseded by meaningless mainstream pop. Society is portrayed as a mess of power, greed and abuse. The gangsters are running the show. Patriotism, war, capitalism and religion are tools they deploy. Meanwhile, the ordinary people work themselves to death in factories, are hungry and destitute and Bob is sitting in the kitchen ruminating on life and death. Phew!

'It Takes a Lot to Laugh, It Takes a Train to Cry' (Bob Dylan)
The pace slows right down for this number and the band has a much lighter touch, though that same new sound is still evident. The song is in the key of Ab major and is based around the chords G, C, F and D to create a lazy, laid-back feel. Paul Griffin provides some sparkling piano that dominates the track (quite different to Bob's usual thumped-out piano chords), while Bobby Greg creates the spine with a steady drumbeat perching on the offbeat, ably assisted by Harvey Brooks on bass. Mike Bloomfield's noodling guitar is much more subdued and pushed back in the mix. In between verses, Bob adds a scintillating harmonica break of slurry elongated notes.

The lyrics have been plucked from old blues numbers by Leroy Carr, Brownie McGhee and Charlie Patton, added to and adapted to create something entirely different – a tale of world-weariness and sexuality all jumbled together. The wistfulness comes across as Dylan portrays himself restlessly sitting up all night, lonely and bereft, yearning for adventure, yearning for love. He wants to be riding that freight and making love to his girl. He's feeling trapped. His life, the whole of society, and his girl are all lost. The compasses have been smashed. It's careering into nowhere. He yearns for that perfect partnership.

An earlier attempt at recording this song was called 'Phantom Engineer'. Versions of this can be heard on *The Bootleg Series Volumes 1-3 (Rare & Unreleased) 1961-1991* and *The Bootleg Series Vol. 7: No Direction Home*. These earlier versions are much faster and more guitar-based. The lyrics are slightly different, with the lines about the compasses being smashed emphasising the futility.

'From a Buick 6' (Bob Dylan)

The pace picks up again for this animated blues number in the key of C major. It may be based on Sleepy John Estes's 'Milk Cow Blues', but you wouldn't know it. The repeating guitar riff is augmented with a boisterous bass, driving drumbeat and wailing harmonica, with Kooper's organ filling all the gaps.

Dylan's in a mess. He's sick, strung-out, messed up, pestered and broken. He is tormented with sycophants, businessmen, hangers-on, fans who all want a part of him. He can't get no peace! He is in need of protection and healing.

His head is whirling with ideas, worries and thoughts that are driving him crazy:

Well, you know I need a steam shovel, mama, to keep away the dead
I need a dump truck, baby, to unload my head
She brings me everything and more, and just like I said

He's just met Sara. She's his saviour; his junkyard angel, his soulful mama. She strides in with a swagger, strong, capable and nurturing. She provides refuge.

'Ballad of a Thin Man' (Bob Dylan)

This track stands out as something completely different. The sound created is like nothing else. It's a slow piano-based number in the key of B minor with a plodding rhythm and ethereal organ. The rest of the band is set back in the mix; the result is mysterious and ephemeral.

The lyrics are quite straightforward and aimed at a straight British reporter in 1963 who was trying to understand a musician who was straight out of the Bohemian culture of 1960s Greenwich Village. It's a put-down. Even though the musician is completely naked, telling it like it was, utterly honest, the reporter, who was well educated, intelligent and knowledgeable, cannot understand any of it. He's out of his depth. For him, it's all a freak show of midgets, sword-swallowers and geeks. What he doesn't understand is that the culture has changed and left him high and dry. He and his paltry world and conservative values are the geeks now. He needs to get out of the doorway.

At this time, the counterculture was getting in full swing and there was widespread distrust of all authority figures, be they in government, schools or institutions. The world of the counterculture was based on more hedonistic values and fun coupled with a search for something deeper and more meaningful. Straight culture was decidedly thin and dull, hypocritical and bland. Mr Jones represented all of that boring narrow-minded conservative

culture. Bob visited this place before with 'The Times They Are A-Changin'';
the world of the hipster is a complete mystery to straight culture.

'Queen Jane Approximately' (Bob Dylan)
The song is based around the chords F, E, D and C and uses a jangly piano,
with a wailing organ over a solid bed of guitar and drums. The result is a
mid-paced swirling sound over which Bob delivers his observations and
advice, a kind of psychedelic melange.

It takes the form of a series of comments that almost form a letter from a
kindly, more knowing friend who is spelling out the situation and saying that
when 'she' wakes up to what is going down, he will be there for her.

So who is this Queen Jane? Dylan has mischievously claimed it was a
man. I think it's most probably Joan Baez, but it could be another of his
female acquaintances or even himself. There is also the likelihood, as with
many Dylan compositions, that it is a fusion of a number of people. There is
certainly a connection with how he himself was feeling at the time.

When 'she' has broken ties with family, even become disillusioned with
'herself' and everything 'she's' creating; when 'she' is sick of the sycophants
and the circus surrounding 'her', has realised that the businessmen are
all out for themselves and that the business is run by a bunch of crooked
sharks, then it's time for a genuine relationship, somewhere 'she' can just
be themselves outside of the act. Then, when life has become a mundane,
meaningless grind, it's time to get real. 'She' can come to him for comfort.

'Highway 61 Revisited' (Bob Dylan)
After the rich musical embroidery, we are tossed into a more straightforward
driving blues as the band put their foot down and unleash this blast of sound.
The tempo is manic as they let it all loose in the key of B major and charge
through the chords A, D and E. The siren adds to and accentuates the party
mood. The music reflects the playful light-heartedness of the lyrics, which
deceptively obscure a more sinister meaning.

It starts with what appears to be a biblical reference, except that Abraham
is the name of Dylan's father, so he is the son who was about to be
sacrificed. We are looking here at Bob's escape from his father's conservative
grip and mundane life in a small town. Abraham was a hard-working man
who ran a hardware shop. If he'd had his way, Bob might have ended up
serving customers instead of writing songs.

Highway 61 is the thoroughfare littered with the musical history of America
and this track is strewn with their characters. This is the highway that Dylan
used to mythologise about. It developed a fantastical nature that reflected
American culture. It symbolised his way out of that small-town life. The
road is the journey taken through history from the biblical inanities of God
demanding the murder of a son to the commercialism of nuclear war. It's a
country of great inequality, poverty and ignorance, run by crooks and valuing

shallow beauty. Dylan takes us from the superstition of blind belief to a world where everything has a price, but nothing has any value.

The dire message is tied up in humour. America has sold its soul. The roving gamblers who run the place are prepared to sacrifice billions of people just to make a buck. Immorality rules.

'Just Like Tom Thumb's Blues' (Bob Dylan)

The chord interplay between E, D, C and G enables some intricate interactions between the guitar and two sonically contrasting types of piano, resulting in a fabulous tight, fun-sounding number that gives the impression of being effortlessly laid-back when it is anything but. The bright steady percussion fills the right-hand side while the complex bass pattern holds centre stage. The sound melds together to form a languid lascivious soulfulness, a moan of desolation. Bob's vocal is slightly off-key and slurry, sounding as worn-out and beat as the lyrics suggest as he delivers the six verses. Even the harmonica breaks sound completely wasted.

Set in Juarez, a Mexican border town just over the Rio Grande from El Paso Texas, a lawless bohemian centre of hedonism, poverty and excess where a man could get lost in a cacophony of vices, temptations and torrid experiences. A place popular with young soldiers, who, having finished their training, take a 'vacation' drinking, whoring and drug-taking before heading off to Vietnam, Iraq or wherever. Even the toughest bikers found the pace soul-destroying.

Easter is a religious festival – the Day of the Dead – where the depravity of the underworld becomes intermingled with religious iconography, devout belief and superstition. A heady mix. The drug cartels run the dope dens, drinking dens and bawdy houses. The police take their bribes and stay out of it. The protagonist (Dylan) is thrown into the midst of this intoxicating confusion. He's chased the American dream of fortune and fame, achieved it and found it empty and unfulfilling. Disillusioned, he is searching for something more and finds it's making him even sicker and has to get out.

The title is not, as Dylan once suggested, based on some painter who lived near the city and had a blue period (rather like Picasso), neither is it about the diminutive child's story character; it, along with some of the borrowed lyrics, stems from Rimbaud. The story mirrors Malcolm Lowry's *Under the Volcano* (whose best friend is the doctor). The nightmarish, druggy/drunken debauchery harkens to the Kerouac Mexican experiences outlined in his road novel *On the Road* while the reference to Poe's *The Murders in Rue Morgue Avenue* adds to the sense of lawlessness and danger.

Bob manages to parade a set of characters, communicate a semblance of the chaos and muddled consciousness and yet spice it all with a garnishing of wry humour.

'Desolation Row' (Bob Dylan)

The two guitars feed off each other, one strumming chords while the other picks an elaborate Spanish-sounding refrain, as we launch into this acoustic Magnus Opus, an eleven-minute epic to end the album. A tour de force of music, poetry and imagery.

The guitars, in drop C tuning with capos on the fourth fret, blend into an airy lightness that is at odds with the subject matter, yet perfectly captures the mood. The track was tried out as an electric number but did not work as magically as this.

Bob is the observer/narrator, peering out disbelievingly at the surreal goings on in this unreal society. In an acid-drenched lysergic vision, he portrays the denizens of this world as bizarre caricatures of historic villains, fairy tale people, musicians, film icons and biblical characters, all grotesquely twisted. His vocal is clear and expressive as he leads us through this poetic excavation of Western culture. The delivery is laconic and detached as he takes the part of a narrator describing the scenes without judgement.

The poetry, which has achieved new heights, is another Beat-driven indictment of our crazy culture, heavily influenced by Allen Ginsberg and very Burroughs-ish in its druggy depictions. He's peering through the veneer of civilisation into the subterranean reality of society. Through a sequence of incidents strewn with metaphor and illusion, he peels back the layers through strata of bizarre illustrations to reveal the decaying core.

The piece starts with a reference to the lynching of three black men, in Duluth (near where Dylan grew up), who came with the circus and were accused of raping a white woman. It is systematic of the intrinsic evil in our society that postcards of the atrocity were gleefully sold. Bob takes us above the pettiness of civil rights, anti-war and politics. It doesn't matter which side you're on when the whole caboodle is sinking. The rottenness is systematic. Everything is corrupt.

This is an extrapolation of Kerouac's *Desolation Angels* in which the whole mess of straight society is portrayed as a mixture of fairy-tale, surreal imagery and reality mixed into a nightmarish fantasy. As biblical figures clash with Shakespearian heroes and heroines, poets brawl in the seat of power where *The Wasteland* meets *The Cantos*. Flawed philosophies stemming from commercialism, capitalism, superstition and power lust create this anarchic confusion.

Singles
'Like a Rolling Stone' b/w 'Gates of Eden'

Both tracks lifted straight off the album. This was the single that proved the real breakthrough in America, going straight to the top of the charts and propelling Bob to another level. He had finally arrived as a fully-fledged international rock star. Bob Dylan the folkie troubadour, was firmly in the past. The snarling, tousle-haired, polka-dotted, dark-glassed hipster was strutting in his place.

'Positively Fourth Street' b/w 'From a Buick 6'

'Positively Fourth Street' was the snarling, sneering put-down of the Greenwich Village folk crew who had turned on him after he had gone electric. The vitriol towards the backstabbing jealousy was extreme. Bob had a way with words.

The song has a pop sensibility which is why it was left off the album and reserved as a single. As the band shuffle along in the same vein as on the album, the organ tends to dominate. It proved sufficient to propel it into the top ten on both sides of the pond and cement his status as a rock star.

For a long time, this was my favourite Dylan track. I greatly appreciated the acerbic put-downs and clever lyrics.

'Can You Please Crawl Out Your Window' b/w 'Highway 61 Revisited'

This track was recorded with The Hawks but had a similar feel to the last one. It is just as vitriolic, full of sneering put-downs and arrogance, but this time the complex G, C, D, B and A chords don't work as smoothly to create the pop feel. It's a jerky rendition that proved nowhere near as popular, only appearing in the lower regions of the charts. Even so, there is a lot to admire, with Richard Manuel's jangly piano and Garth Hudson's swirling organ. Robbie Robertson brings a different dimension of guitar to that of Mike Bloomfield – less bluesy and strident. Bob sings it a little tongue-in-cheek, sweetening the acid with a hint of humour.

This was the track that brought to a head the difficult relationship with his rival Phil Ochs. Phil had reputedly liked 'Positively Fourth Street', but when Bob asked him about the new single, Phil told him that it wasn't as good. That elicited an argument and Bob kicked him out of the car. Many harsh words were spoken, some of which were reported in the press, and a rift was opened that never fully healed.

The song is written in terms of advice to a woman trapped in an abusive, controlling relationship. Bob is telling her to get out and live, the guy is useless and it's not going anywhere. The ambiguous darkness awaits.

The speculation is that this is aimed at Edie Sedgewick and Andy Warhol. Bob had become involved with Edie and Warhol's Factory.

Blonde on Blonde (1966)

Personnel:
Bob Dylan: guitar, piano, vocals and harmonica
Bill Atkins: keyboards
Wayne Butler: trombone
Kenneth Buttrey: drums
Rick Danko: bass
Bobby Greg: drums
Paul Griffin: piano
Jerry Kennedy: guitar
Al Kooper: organ, guitar
Charlie McCoy: bass, guitar, harmonica, trumpet
Wayne Moss: guitar, vocals
Hargus 'Pig' Robbins: piano, keyboards
Robbie Robertson: guitar, vocals
Henry Strzelecki: bass
Joe South: bass, guitar
Jerry schatzberg: photography
Bob Johnson: producer
Label: Colombia
Recorded at Colombia Studio A and Colombia Studio B Nashville
Release date: June 1966
Highest chart positions: UK: 3 US: 9

This double album was the culmination of the musical and poetic
development that had taken place throughout the electric period. By now,
Bob had a clear idea of the sound he wanted to create. He later called it a
'thin, wild mercury sound'. He had something to aim for.

This Dylan was a slightly different version. He was in a good and a bad
place. He had a good thing going with Sara Lownds (formerly Shirley Marlin
Noznisky), a dark-haired, big-eyed model. They had started seeing each other
romantically in 1964 and in November 1965, while still embroiled with both
Joan and Edie, he had secretly and unexpectedly married Sara. In the midst
of all the turmoil, chaos and jagged relationships, it seems that he had found
a rock to hang on to. She was to be the muse for a number of his greatest
songs. The bad place was that he was strung out on a number of different
drugs. Bob was smoking marijuana for pleasure, dropping acid, taking
uppers to keep going, downers to get back to earth and had developed a
heroin habit. Then there was the alcohol and nicotine: 'I got very strung out
for a while. I kicked the habit. I had a $25-a-day habit and I kicked it.' It was
a state of affairs that could not go on.

At first, his marriage did not seem to elicit any change in behaviour. Bob
continued with exactly the same womanising and pill-popping lifestyle
as before. He was not besotted enough to be averse to leaving her for six

months while he went on the road. Perhaps the marriage had merely been precipitated by Sara becoming pregnant? Perhaps there was a delayed effect not to be fully realised until after his motorbike accident? Perhaps it was the birth of his first child that precipitated a profound change in Bob? Whatever, this marriage was to exert a major change in Bob in the coming months – but not yet.

After the recording of *Highway 61*, Bob put together a permanent backing band to go on tour with. As neither Kooper nor Bloomfield liked the idea of touring, he approached The Hawks, Ronnie Hawkins's backing band. They were seasoned performers and that was the start of a long and fruitful relationship.

The historic tour of the UK and Ireland with The Hawks was once again documented on the controversial 'fly on the wall' documentary *Don't Look Back*. Despite its massive importance as a historic documentation of Bob at his peak with the powerful Hawks, the full footage of the live performances and associated documentary material have never been released though tantalising excerpts have turned up and bootleg copies (including a sequence of a burned-out, exhausted, strung-out Dylan sharing a taxi with John Lennon) have found their way out.

The Hawks were first used in the studio on the single 'Can You Please Crawl Out Your Window' and when it came to recording the next album, he got them into the studio in New York. Somehow it did not work out. Much as they tried, through a number of sessions, Bob could not achieve the sound he was after. Bob Johnson, with opposition from Albert Grossman, suggested moving to Nashville and using the highly experienced session musicians they had there. That worked.

At least we have the most amazing album *Blonde on Blonde,* courtesy of Nashville, but I can't help asking myself what might have been if, following Albert Grossman's edict, they had stuck with the far harder sound coming out of the musicians in New York. We might have been saved from all that country crap that clogged up the next few albums with that ear-aching saccharin-coated crooning. Bob might have been saved from himself. The future would have been very different. But at least we had *Blonde on Blonde*.

This was the height of Bob's fame and also the period of greatest pressure. Albert had him touring, writing *Tarantula*, contracted to producing albums and singles, nonstop promotions, photo shoots and interviews. Then there was the standard to live up to. Everything he produced was analysed and questioned. He had to keep coming up with the goods. The treadmill never stopped.

One of the results of this immense pressure was that the songs had dried up. Where once he had gone into the studio with a bunch of new songs, leaving behind a trail of unused outtakes, this time he fell short. Bob found himself writing songs in the studio while the musicians sat around for hours waiting. It certainly did not seem to affect the quality, though. The album turned out to be his best and has not been bettered to this day. Bob had achieved the mammoth task of fusing his complex musical vision to his surreal, bohemian poetry. He realised his hipster's dream and brought to life characters he had plucked out of the New York streets, infusing them with fantasy.

Little did we know that this was to be the last glimpse we'd see of Bob Dylan, the James Dean hipster in shades for some while due to his motorbike accident six days after the release of the album, conveniently removing all the contractual obligations. The rumour mill went into overtime. There had been no accident; he was in rehab in the Chelsea Hotel. He was dead. The accident had disfigured him so that he'd never appear in public again. His larynx was crushed and he'd never sing. Little, if any was true. The accident was probably less severe than reported. He had mounted the pavement and come off his bike while coming out of Albert Grossman's drive. Albert and Sally Grossman had been following him and found him on the ground groaning. He had done some damage to his neck, but it probably wasn't broken. He did not go to hospital but convalesced in the basement of a doctor friend called Ed Thaler, who lived in Woodstock.

In 1966, the counterculture that Bob had inspired with his six amazing acoustic and electric albums (I pass on the debut) was exploding. The civil rights movement and anti-war movement were gathering force. Fellow musicians from Greenwich Village like Phil Ochs and Joan Baez were heavily involved. The music scene was exploding into a creative supernova with psychedelia, heavy metal, blues, folk rock, folk, poetry, jazz fusion and world music. Bob went missing.

During 1966, he did go into rehab at some stage (which was where he wrote Sara for his wife), but as to when that was is a little unclear. One thing is certain: he hung out in Woodstock, resting and recuperating, playing for fun with The Band and rehearsing in his own basement and the house The Band lived in called Big Pink. The man that re-emerged seemed to be a different man. The sound that came out of those relaxed sessions, released as *The Basement Tapes* was completely different. The poetry was different. The whole social/political vibe was different. The hipster had evaporated.

For once, the album contained no liner notes or poetry. It came out as a double album in a gatefold cover. On the front was a slightly blurry photo of Bob, clean-shaven, tousle-haired in scarf and jacket. Inside, a collage of photos. The title came out of a late-night brainstorm with everyone firing names. There is the acronym BoB, the Brian Jones and Anita Pallenberg theory, two blonde lesbians?

Blonde on Blonde was the last of the wondrous electric trilogy that lit up the sixties. We weren't to hear anything reaching close to these heights again for many years to come. Indeed, it wasn't until *Planet Waves* and *Blood on the Tracks* in 1974 and 1975 that we saw a true return to form. His legacy was left, though and *Blonde on Blonde* was a sparkling jewel.

'Rainy Day Women #12 & 35' (Bob Dylan)

We're off to a fun start to the album with this chaotic rambunctious performance. No so much thin mercury as drunken mariachi. It's like being at the fairground and all the drunken punters have stolen instruments and are letting fly with real gusto. Not too far off the mark, either.

Rainy day women was street slang for marijuana and Bob, at this time, was greatly into dope. I don't hold with any biblical 'stoning' interpretation. That simply does not make sense, especially when you take into account the way this was recorded. Bob wrote the lyrics and created a simple E, A, B chord progression. The whole band then got completely wasted, swapped instruments and had a great time playing it. The song is accompanied with shouts, whoops and laughs. It lurches and chugs along in gleeful stoned euphoria. They decided to keep the chaotic live take as it was, a fabulous, riotous start to the album. A good time was had by all.

Incredibly it was released as a single and, despite the obvious drug reference (probably not understood by conservative radio), received good airplay and took Dylan to the top of the charts on both sides of the pond.

'Pledging My Time' (Bob Dylan)

After the gaiety of the first track, we're brought down to earth with this druggy blues. It's a standard blues around the A, D and E chords. There are shades of Elmore James's 'It Hurts Me Too' and a little lyrical inspiration from Robert Johnson's 'Come On in My Kitchen'. Bob sings it as a sombre number with lots of wailing harmonica. Robbie Robertson provides the slow bluesy pace and Hagus Robbins supplies the piano in the background.

The song is drenched in desperation with a sense of futility. They've been drinking (shooting up?) all day in some nightclub? at a party? At a friend's place? And now he's feeling sick. His girl has gone off with some jerk and he's making a connection but really can't be bothered. Still, he is willing to make a commitment of sorts. The place is an accident waiting to happen and he has to get out. He doesn't want to leave without her, but he does – just hoping that she gets out of there too.

The song was released in edited form as the B-side of 'Rainy Day Women #12 & 35'.

'Visions of Johanna' (Bob Dylan)

The track was originally called 'Freeze Out' when they attempted to record it in New York with The Hawks. Bob had a vision of how it should sound but could not manage to get the band to perform in the way he wanted. They were too hard-edged. He wanted something smoother and gentler yet retaining some harder elements. He finally achieved what he wanted in Nashville, with Joe South providing a throbbing base and Robbie coming up with the occasional hard blast of guitar.

The song is played in the key of A major with the capo on the second fret, the chords being G, C and D. A strummed acoustic sets the softer tone while the band, with Al Kooper's organ, create a mellow, late-night feel that conjures up a lonely night sitting up in the hotel room thinking about life and the characters that have been part of his world. Bob's voice drawls, wallowing in the melancholy as the snare drum beats out a compelling rhythm and Bob's harmonica cries mournfully. The music gels into a solid amalgam, conveying the lateness of the hour, surroundings and mood.

Bob was living in a room in the Chelsea Hotel at the time – an old creaking hotel that has been the residence of writers, poets and musicians down the years. Dylan Thomas stayed there, as did Henry Miller and later on, Jimi Hendrix, Janis Joplin, Patti Smith, Sid Vicious and Leonard Cohen. The hotel was a ramshackle bohemian haunt full of artworks and gurgling pipes. It had character.

Sara was pregnant and one can imagine Bob alone in the room, listening to lovers, gurgling pipes and voices in the hallway. The poetry has reached its most eloquent imagery, reflecting the underground bohemian life in New York with its hookers and dealers contrasting the middle-aged theatre-goers, creating pictures in the mind full of intrigue. There's the mysterious Johanna, who may well be Joan Baez, as might the Madonna who has still not showed but who is escaping her cage, the street-wise Louise, little boy lost and the all-knowing fiddler.

The poem contains some of Bob's most outstanding lines: 'The ghost of 'lectricity howls in the bones of her face' and 'Oh, jewels and binoculars hang from the head of the mule'. I am always amused by a couple of the lines: 'The country music station plays soft but there's nothing, really nothing to turn off' – which is a reflection on the shallowness of the music of the day. The irony being that within a short time, Bob would be producing music of a similar ilk. Then there is: 'Inside the museums, Infinity goes up on trial. Voices echo, this is what salvation must be like after a while' – which I interpret as a prod at religion and its promise of eternal salvation. The irony here again being that Bob would throw himself headlong into religion in the late seventies and fully adopt the idea of everlasting life – funny how things change.

'One of Us Must Know (Sooner or Later)' (Bob Dylan)
This was the only song to emerge from the multiples New York sessions, having taken 24 takes, and was released as the first single – strangely not going anywhere. That was peculiar because it possessed a very haunting melody and had quite a hook. Perhaps it was just too slow?

The song is in the key of F major with a capo on the fifth fret. At the time, it was nowhere near finished and Bob worked feverishly to both write and work out the arrangement in the studio where they were recording. He didn't even have the chorus. The end result was worth it. The harmonica break leads into a cool backing with the piano driving the band and organ wafting ethereally over the top as the drums perform jazz figures to hold it together. The result is very atmospheric. Bob's voice is heavy with emotion and expression, full of remorse, soaring and falling as the band builds to a climax for the chorus and drops off back into the verses.

The song is a reflection on a failed relationship in which many harsh words were spoken. It's heavy with regrets. I am reminded of that scene from the documentary *Don't Look Back* when a bereft Joan Baez makes her exit: 'I didn't mean to treat you so bad. You don't have to take it so personal. I didn't mean to make you so sad. You just happened to be there, that's all.'

'I Want You' (Bob Dylan)
A boisterous, rousing track that's more about lost lust than lost love. The song is in the key of F major (capo on the fifth fret) and runs through the chords C, E, A and G to create an infectious hook that draws you in. It begins with a clattering snare drum as Bob's harmonica plays the tuneful melody. The guitar picks up a light, breezy refrain that sounds playful, joyful, and at odds with the lyrics. The repeating chorus is extremely captivating; Bob's voice is dripping with naked yearning, relaxed and full of inflexion. No wonder they selected it as an early single. Surprisingly it was only a modest hit.

Once again, we are plunged into a surreal pantomime universe inhabited by a weird cast of characters. These denizens of the subterranean world that Dylan inhabits include guilty undertakers, lonesome organ grinders, drunken politicians, weeping mothers, sleeping saviours, the Queen of Spades, chamber maids and a dancing child (Brian Jones?). Are they mourning a lost love? Cracked bells and Chinese flutes? The world isn't working properly anymore. Everything is flawed. It's over. He wants her back. There's more than love in this. He wants her with an animal passion. Is it Edie Sedgewick? Anita Pallenburg? Or Bob Hankering after his universal muse?

'Stuck Inside of Mobile With the Memphis Blues Again' (Bob Dylan)
A track in the key of E major that is more of a country rock than blues. The rasping harmonica leads in before the rest of the band enter, their sound epitomising that heavy, fluid sound that Bob referred to as his thin, wild mercury sound. The drums set up a fast snare pace and the throbbing bass underpins the whole song. Al Kooper's organ is very dominant in its high-pitched background wail with lots of frills and trills, but it's the guitar, with its sublime repeating licks bubbling up through the mix, that steals the show.

A confused Bob is stranded in this dystopian limbo while this surreal urban circus takes place in the mad confusion that surrounds him. Suspended in unreality, the disbelief and bewilderment permeate the fabric of the song as exotic historical, fictional and biblical characters perform their bizarre acts.

The verses are each cameos of the extraordinary, brief tales and interludes from lives with all their strange behaviours. The lysergic-induced fantasy, that is reality, is full of people getting uglier when the medicines are mixed, corrupt senators handing out their bribes, megalomaniac preachers, poets in the alley and exotic dancers who not only know what you need but 'know what you want'. The 'folkie' Dylan from Alabama is stuck in the wrong place with this rock and blues from Memphis! Bob told Robert Shelton that the ragman was Satan.

Once again, it seems that Bob liked borrowing and adapting words as well as music. 'I Wish I Was a Mole in the Ground' was a song by Bascom Lamar Lunsford (a traditional Appalachian country singer) that featured the lines 'Cause railroad man they'll kill you when he can and drink your blood like wine'. The song was covered by Jackson C Frank.

Although it took 20 takes, with much revising of lyrics and arrangement, the end result is as mind-blowing as the lyrics.

'Leopard-Skin Pill-Box Hat' (Bob Dylan)

We move from the esoteric to the ridiculous with this stomping blues deploying chords A, D and E. In the same vein as 'Rainy Day Women #12 And 35', it rattles along with much hilarity. The track is a classic twelve-bar blues arrangement with walking bass and a lurching beat. It starts with some great opening lead guitar from Bob. The later string-melting guitar break from Robbie Robertson is incandescent. The song may be loosely based on the Lightnin' Hopkins track 'Automobile Blues'.

It pillories the fashion sense of a wealthy socialite attempting to copy the trend set up by Jackie Kennedy, who was photographed wearing a new trendy pillbox hat. The ridicule is aimed at Edie Sedgwick, with whom Bob had a fling (resulting in an abortion) before she moved on to Bob Neuwirth. From my perspective, this isn't so much a vicious put-down as a fun, sarcastic romp. There's no malice in it. The song is full of hilarious lyrical images such as 'like a mattress balancing on a bottle of wine'.

Late in the year, it was released as the fifth single from the album but only reached 81 on the US charts. Not surprising, really, by this time, most people already had it on the album.

'Just Like a Woman' (Bob Dylan)

A sad, beautiful song that was aimed at Edie Sedgwick. Bob not only had a fling with her but a serious love affair. She was a very wealthy socialite who had become embroiled in the Andy Warhol 'Factory'. Bob was introduced to Andy Warhol when he was on the way up and was looking for anything that would give him attention. He did not get on with Andy but he was hungry for fame, love and adventure and was greatly attracted to Edie. Most of *Blonde on Blonde* was revolving around their love affair. Edie became a lost tragic figure, had an abortion following her affair with Bob and died in 1971. She was vulnerable and used; life in 'The Factory' gobbled her up. Bob was compassionately observing her diminution from outside. 'The Factory' was her world. Her drug use and desperation to fit in were destroying her. The song is full of the drug slang that was associated with the 60s culture of the New York scene – from amphetamines, fog and Queen Jane.

This incredibly melodic track starts with some wistful harmonica, clattering snare and wafting organ. It's such a delicate number. The bridge featuring sensitively plucked guitar leading to rising organ is simply delightful. Bob's vocal is so etched with sadness – haunting. The harmonica-suffused outro is magnificent.

'Most Likely You Go Your Way I'll Go Mine' (Bob Dylan)
This faster pop-orientated rock track has a superb melody that pulls you in and makes for a great way to open side three. Bob's drawling vocal is hypnotic. It's in the key of G major with a multitude of minor chords around B, A, C and F (in the middle eight) creating a bouncy rock song. The pedestrian bass, acting as a pathfinder, holds it together and all the instruments gel as the repeating refrain congeals into a compelling sound. Everything melds together to produce a solid wall of sound. The outro, with Bob's harp, is wonderful.

This is another track about the break-up with Edie. Bob has moved on to form a relationship with Sara but still looks back with sadness, regret and a touch of bitterness. He had become fed up with her changing feelings, lies and duplicity. She's behaved badly and though she's sorry, he's had enough. She may be full of remorse, but it's time to split.

'Temporary Like Achilles' (Bob Dylan)
This track started life as a fragment known as 'Medicine Sunday' and progressed into other incarnations. The music is a slow, simmering blues based around the chords G, C minor, D and F minor. What makes it different is the unexpected chord changes. The piece is essentially a piano number with a light shuffling snare and the guitar playing off the piano.

Lyrically straightforward compared to many of the ambiguous surreal offerings on the album, it is still, nonetheless, embellished with a few of Bob's obfuscations and quirks. On the surface, it tells the tale of a lover's tiff with the protagonist, desperate to get back with his lover. However, she's locked him out, had him barred and doesn't want him coming around anymore. As to who this is about, that's anyone's guess. Is this a throwback to Suze with the scorpion as her sister? Who is this Achilles? Certainly, the circus and Achilles in the alley bring to mind Andy Warhol's Factory, which means that this could be the bust-up with Edie Sedgwick. Then the title suggests that Dylan is Achilles – temporarily having a weakness that he'll get over.

'Absolutely Sweet Marie' (Bob Dylan)
Another up-tempo blues number that gallops along fairly. The song is in Eb major with interesting chord experimentation around A, B, C minor

and G minor. Careering like a mad freight, the organ and drums create a bouncy, jaunty feel with their boisterous interaction. Despite the frustration communicated by the lyrics, there is a playfulness to the tune and Bob sings it expressively in a slurred voice that emphasises that intrinsic humour. There is even an exuberant harmonica break towards the end.

The lyrics are mischievous, full of sexual imagery, with Bob 'beating on his trumpet' 'with a fever down in his pockets'. As always, he's picking lines randomly from memory, from films or old blues songs and altering them, adapting them, stitching them together. For instance, the infamous line that associated him with the sixties counterculture 'to live outside the law you must be honest' was adapted from the 1958 film *The Line Up* while the line about white horses is straight out of many blues classics.

The picture you get is of a frustrated drunken Bob being stood up by this mysterious Marie. So who was she? Is this Edie (rhymes with Marie), Joan or a fictitious lover?

'4th Time Around' (Bob Dylan)

A delightful, delicate song about a love affair that has turned sour, the use of the key of E major with an arrangement based around the chords C, F, E and D creates a light, breezy feel. It starts with delicately picked guitars accompanied by Bob's melancholy harmonica playing before the drums enter with a fast military beat and the fabulous, slow, throbbing bass underpins the production. Bob's vocal is sad and mournful as he relates the tale of being castigated and thrown out into the street, coming back for a strange reencounter resulting in her fainting and him rummaging through her drawers, before filling a shoe with her Jamaican rum and taking it to her? Or to someone else?

The Beatles had released *Rubber Soul* and this song was a response to Lennon's 'Norwegian Wood'. The two songs share a similar melody and description of an affair. When Dylan played the song to John, he became very paranoid, thinking that the last lines were a warning from Bob to John not to 'steal' his songwriting technique. Later he came to believe that it was probably a playful homage.

'Obviously 5 Believers' (Bob Dylan)

We end side three with a blistering twelve-bar blues in the key of D major using a progression of chords A, D and E. A standard blues that is modelled on Memphis Minnie's 'Chauffeur Blues' that really allows the band to let rip. Right from the start, the strident guitar sets the scene with a recurrent riff while the chuntering rhythm section hammers along. The sound is more reminiscent of *Highway 61* than *Blonde on Blonde*. Great to listen to but little more than a gutsy blues workout for the band.

Dylan is working well within himself for this number but still comes up with a magical vocal performance, demonstrating the range of his vocal abilities. The lyrics are simple; he's repeating lines in the classic blues manner, calling for his lover to please come home, reassuring her that it's all good. Of course, he throws a bunch of jugglers, believers and her mama into the mix to keep it interesting.

'Sad-Eyed Lady of the Lowlands' (Bob Dylan)

Side four is just one track – but what a track! 'Sad Eyed Lady of the Lowlands' is an epic eleven minutes and 22 seconds of majestic, sublime mastery. Everything came together to create a distillation of all that Bob had been about during this period. In the key of D major, with the capo on the second fret, utilising the chords C, G, F and D, he set out to produce the ultimate love song to his recent bride Sara Lownds. Bob tried to gather all his romantic imagery into one song. Once he'd started, he couldn't stop. Shortly after recording it, Bob told Robert Shelton that 'This is the best song I've ever written'. I wouldn't go that far but it's pretty high up on the list.

On the later track 'Sara', Bob claimed that he'd stayed up for days writing the song for her. The truth was that it was largely written in eight hours in the studio in Nashville. Bob sat in the corner and wrote it in one long splurge while the musicians played cards. In the early hours of the morning, he brought them all together, ran through the arrangement and recorded it. When the band started playing the piece, they had no idea how long it was and kept building up to a finale, only to find that there were many more verses still to come.

The piece starts with strummed guitar, a steady, largely unembellished drum and a pensive harmonica. The organ follows the melody, swirling with flourishes and emphasising the chorus. It's all very slow and repetitive and yet it works. It provides the platform for Bob's poetic imagery, a eulogy for Sara that sounds more like a hymn than a festive celebration. The romance is there, but the presentation is solemn and reverential. Bob enthused to Jules Siegel 'just listen to that! That's old-time carnival music!' – I don't know about that. It doesn't sound positive enough to be any carnival I've ever been to; it's far too deferential for that.

As for the lyrics, they take the form of ten verses of poetry broken up by a chorus every second verse. Lines of verse list her virtues and end in unanswered questions geared to pique our curiosity. It's full of enigmatic imagery, cryptic descriptions and elusive phrases. Some of it is possible to dissect; the rest just sets an emotional setting. Bob is placing Sara on a pedestal and adoring her.

The use of lowlands is similar to Lownds. Her father was a scrap metal dealer hence the line 'sheet metal memories of cannery row'. Then there's mention of her first husband who was a magazine photographer – 'your magazine husband who one day just had to go'.

It shouldn't have worked. It was too long, too pedestrian and the lyrics too obtuse, yet it did. The ethereal atmosphere carried it, the sentiment swamped it, the melody ate at you and those eleven minutes and 22 seconds absorbed you. This was Dylan at the peak of his powers. That vocal was narcotic. Once you'd sampled it, you were hooked. Like all good poetry, the contents communicated even when the words made no sense.

It took four takes to get it right. It was not only the end of the album, the end of a trilogy of superb ground-breaking electric albums; it was the end of an era. Although there were other highs to look forward to, this was the end of this golden period.

Outtakes

Because of the way Bob was working on this album, trying things out in the studio, reworking lyrics and arrangements, using different bands in New York and then Nashville and making numerous takes of each song (sometimes as many as 30 takes before he was satisfied) there are hundreds of outtakes. Many of these were gathered together (along with outtakes from *Bringing it All Back Home* and *Highway 61 Revisited*) and released as *The Bootleg Series Vol. 12: The Cutting Edge 1965-1966*.

For those who can't stomach eighteen CDs of numerous repeating takes, there is a six-CD version and if that is still too much, there is a handy 36-track best of that has all the important outtakes and is fabulous.

'I'll Keep it With Mine' (released on The Bootleg Series 1-3) (Bob Dylan)
This demo is a piano piece that uses the chords C/E, F, C/G and F/A to create a heart-wrenching melody that wafts along and draws you into it. One of his best. Bob wrote this for Nico during their brief fling and so it is appropriate that he gave it to her. It suits her breathy delivery. The truth is that the song was out of place here. It was written in 1964 and a demo made for Witmark. A piano recording was attempted in 1965 for the *Bringing it All Back Home* album. They were going to record a full band version for *Blonde on Blonde*, the backing tracks were laid down, but Bob never added the vocals. Shame. I'm not sure it would have suited the album, but it is a great song.

The lyric, sung in a plaintive voice, takes the form of advice from a friend. His girl is restless, searching for something she already has, searching for love, but she could stay with him; it's there. She could add her love to his. She's leaving, but she can come back any time. She needs to stop beating herself up.

'I Wanna Be Your Lover' (Released on *Biograph*) (Bob Dylan)
This song, using a drop C tuning, capo on the seventh fret, with the limited chords of C, G and F, was little more than a mad gallop. The hectic pace is sustained through a surreal landscape full of crazy characters. It was one that was recorded in the New York sessions with his hard-edged kick-ass band but never revisited in Nashville.

Bob was showing The Beatles what you could do with poetic imagery. He took 'I Wanna Be Your Man' and jazzed it up into a Daliesque romp. This was the time when he was simply plucking characters out of past blues classics (Jumpin' Judy), Greek Mythology (Phaedra), history (Rasputin) or stuff he'd made up himself. None of it had to make sense. It added to the verbal landscape to create a rich backdrop. He was embellishing his songs to give them a bizarre twist. It worked too.

Back in the seventies, in the days when we Dylan nuts used to exchange tapes, I had this song, along with other outtakes, including 'She's Your Lover Now', on a bootleg tape that I kept in the car and I played it to death.

'Jet Pilot' (released on Biograph) (Bob Dylan)
Just a 49-second fragment of a song idea. It's in the key of E with a simple E, A, B riff similar to the style from *Highway 61 Revisited* and said to be an early working for 'Tombstone Blues' though it sounds a lot different to me. This was recorded in New York with that harder-sounding band.

As for the lyrics, they're wild – some hard-ass trans woman that Dylan used as a comical foil. I'd have liked to have heard it fully developed. Sounds like fun.

'Medicine Sunday' (released on Highway 61 Interactive CD-Rom) (Bob Dylan)
Another fragment of a song that eventually evolved into 'Temporary Like Achilles'. In late 1965, Bob went into the studios with The Hawks to attempt to produce a follow-up single to 'Positively Fourth Street' and start work on the follow-up album to *Highway 61 Revisited*. Bob was using the studio as a way of developing ideas, lyrics and arrangements, trying them out and listening to them back.

The lyrics show Bob's grounding in the blues. Trains were a major element in blues and Bob seemed to like them too. He used trains as a setting for his tales. The girl in the prison, with her hands tied behind her back, is watching the train pull away with a smile. It's a simple metaphor. He's wanting her to leave her man and go off with him. Could this be Edie and the prison of the Factory? Or is it Sara and her husband?

In the end, he abandoned this song, adapted the arrangement and just kept the last line. I think he liked the reversed sexual innuendo of 'Honey, but you're so hard'.

'Number One' (unreleased) (Bob Dylan)
An unreleased outtake that does not appear to have leaked out but is still stashed away in the vaults.

'She's Your Lover Now' (released on Bootleg Series 1-3) (Bob Dylan)
A number on my much-played bootleg tape. I adored the vitriolic put-downs – so acidic. This is a piano composition in C major. There is a bootleg of

Dylan doing a solo piano version which is even more incendiary.

The song reminds me of a scene from *Don't Look Back* featuring Bob confronting Joan with a bunch of her friends and a new lover in a big hat. It is full of the same bitterness and hurt. But this song is probably aimed at Edie Sedgwick.

It's the ultimate put-down song in the extremity of its visible pain, anger and bitterness. The cruelty is immense. It brims with disdain without a hint of compassion.

As a song, it is difficult. There is no hook. It is long, intense and all on one level. But once you get into it, it's compulsive. The chord progression is identical to 'Like a Rolling Stone', but it lacks the hook to break it up. Its complexity and length made it difficult to get right in the studio. Under the title 'Just a Little Glass of Water', it was subject to nineteen takes but produced nothing that Bob was happy with. My version ends with only part of the last verse; following 'Your eyes cry wolf...' the song breaks down.

As it stands, it remains one of Bob's unfinished gems. Parts of the tune were disassembled and used in other songs like 'One of Us Must Know'.

'Lunatic Princess' (released on The Cutting Edge 1965-1966 deluxe edition) (Bob Dylan)
Another fragment of a song that turned up on *The Cutting Edge*. It is subtitled 'Why Do You Have to Be So Frantic' and it is one of Bob's put-down songs that he was busy writing at that time. I think life in general, his failed love affairs, the anger generated at his changes in direction, had made him resentful and bitter (along with the amphetamines). It's a rocker, storming along on an A, D, E riff. Unfortunately, it breaks down after one minute and eighteen seconds and Bob does nothing with it.

Singles
'One of Us Must Know (Sooner or Later)' b/w **'Queen Jane Approximately'** (Bob Dylan)
Lifted straight off the album and hardly dented the charts.

'Rainy Day Women #12 and 35' b/w **'Pledging My Time'** (Bob Dylan)
This was also lifted straight off the album, but this time the carnival feel appealed to radio listeners and took it straight to the top of the charts.

'I Want You' b/w **'Just Like Tom Thumb's Blues'** (recorded live in Liverpool, England, May 14, 1966) (Bob Dylan)
The A-side was off the album, but the B-side was an interesting live recording that had not seen the light of day anywhere else. It made it into the top 20.

'Just Like a Woman' b/w **'Obviously 5 Believers'** (Bob Dylan)
The fourth single lifted from the album. They were trying to get their money's
worth. By this time, a lot of people had the album and did not need the
single. It failed to hit the top 30.

'Leopard-Skin Pill-Box Hat' b/w **'Most Likely You Go Your Way I'll
Go Mine'** (Bob Dylan)
The last single to be lifted from the album. By this time, there were few
people who did not possess the album, so it flopped.

'If You Gotta Go, Go Now' b/w **'To Ramona'** (from Another Side of
Bob Dylan) (Bob Dylan)
At last, we had a single which was a new recording – though who came up
with the idea of putting 'To Ramona', from four albums back, on the B-side?
Strange choice.

This was a lightweight pop song aimed at the charts with its simple three-
chord arrangement around G, C and D. Light-hearted enough, indeed jaunty
and bouncy enough to have been a hit. Good conventional chart material.

The lyrics are probably what prevented it from getting airplay. They were a
cheeky, humorous poke at the pervading prudish conservative values of the
day. The sexual revolution was well underway in Bohemian circles (and Bob
had been right there at the forefront) but in mainstream society, there had
to be a veneer of respectability. Despite the advent of the birth control pill,
sex before marriage was still considered a sin. When Bob was humorously
telling his girl that she was free to do what she liked, but it was time to either
go or stay the night, the radio was not quite ready to allow such brazen
sentiments. One only has to look at the trouble The Rolling Stones had a year
later when they released their 'Let's Spend the Night Together' single, which
was banned. Strangely though, Manfred Mann got away with doing a version
which took them to the top of the charts. The best cover was by Fairport
Convention, who sang it in French and brought it to life.

John Wesley Harding (1967)

Personnel:
Bob Dylan: guitar, piano, vocals and harmonica
Kenneth A. Buttrey: drums
Peter Drake: pedal steel guitar on 'Down Along the Cove' and 'I'll Be Your Baby Tonight'
Charlie McCoy: bass
John Berg: photography
Bob Johnson: producer
Charlie Bragg: engineer
Label: Colombia
Recorded at Colombia Studio B Nashville
Release date: December 1967
Highest chart positions: UK: 1 US: 2

In between *Blonde on Blonde* and *John Wesley Harding*, the universe had changed. The sixties counterculture had exploded. Rock music had gone undergone a massive rocket-propelled flareup. The underground scene had swept into the mainstream. Hallucinogenics had made their impact. Psychedelia, acid rock, progressive rock and electronics had transformed the music business from being single-orientated to album based. The Vietnam War was in full swing, with massive protests and draft card burning. The civil rights movement was also becoming fiery. The black panther movement had sprung up and there were numerous violent marches and protests. It seemed that America was in flames, with the young against the old and this was reflected in the music and lyrics of the time.

Things had changed for Bob too. He was a married man and a child was on the way. At first, this did not seem to impact greatly on his lifestyle, but things soon became a lot different. He had withdrawn into the quieter country air of Woodstock and removed himself from the frantic New York scene. He mellowed out.

Prior to *John Wesley Harding*, Bob had been at the centre of a whirlwind, the crazy hip jester in the midst of a circus entourage, he epitomised cool, yet there were limits to what any man could take. Everyone wanted a bit of him. The pressures were immense. Albert Grossman had lined up tours, contracted him to produce a novel (*Tarantula*) as well as a string of further albums. The media were mad for him with interviews, still annoyingly focussing on his reputation as the 'voice of a generation'. The public, his fans, were incredibly threatening and demanding. There was a constant pressure for him to come up with the goods. Throwing the drugs and mad social whirl into the mix, Dylan had found himself spiralling out of control. Viewed as the coolest dude on the planet, Bob had become stressed beyond belief and had also become disillusioned. The fun had gone. He was looking for a way out.

Following the motorbike accident, he'd found that escape route. The accident effectively put a stop to the aforementioned pressures. He had taken time to reflect and was of the opinion that he no longer wanted to be part of the man-eating, ruthless music business. He'd had enough of being ultra-hip and cool. He turned his back on the 60s scene and was content to bring up his family, relax and enjoy himself. He still made demo recordings and copyrighted songs, though. Some of those found their way to other artists to record – Manfred Mann, Julie Driscoll and Jimi Hendrix were benefactors of his output.

After more than a year out of the limelight, Bob had straightened himself out and gotten some of his appetite back, though he no longer desired to jump straight back into rock star cauldron. He set off to Nashville with a new set of simpler songs to record, none of which had or would appear in any of *The Basement Tapes*. The lyrics were less intricate and had moved away from the surreal imagery of his Beat poetry period. They reflected a more content Dylan, with no desire to reassume the mantle of wild hipster. This time he was intent on doing things his way. Completely bucking the current trends, he wanted a sparse drum and bass arrangement but was persuaded to add the steel guitar. The album was recorded quickly in Nashville with a mellow sound, totally different to that thin, wild mercury sound on *Blonde on Blonde*. Though, perhaps being in two minds, he did ask Robbie Robertson and Garth Hudson to overdub some guitar and keyboard, but they declined, saying they liked it just as it was. Who knows what that would have sounded like if they had contributed? We might have been back to something more resembling that mid-sixties sound? We'll never know.

Bob wanted the album released without any fuss or hype and did not tour to promote it. The only gig that he did in 1968 was a pair of memorial shows for Woody Guthrie in which, accompanied by The Band, he sang three Woody Guthrie songs: 'Grand Coulee Dam', 'Dear Mrs Roosevelt' and 'I Ain't Got No Home'. The next time we'd get to see him perform was at the Isle of Wight festival in 1969.

This had been a hectic period for us. As an eighteen-year-old, I was in the midst of the London underground scene, immersed in the festivals and music. My world revolved around Roy Harper, Jimi Hendrix, Captain Beefheart, Cream, Fleetwood Mac, Pink Floyd and the scene around the burgeoning London underground clubs. We'd missed Bob Dylan and regarded him as a major instigator of what was happening in the music scene as well as in the current social climate with its youth revolution. It had all taken off while he was missing. We were dying to hear what impact he would make. We needed him. What was he going to say about the war and civil rights? What sort of new sound was he going to come out with?

The rumour mill had been rife since his accident. There were tales of him being dead, horribly injured, strung out on heroin, a vegetable with severe head injuries. Now he was releasing a new album. I bought *John Wesley*

Harding on the day of its release. That was a status I afforded very few artists. As a student, money was tight. I generally confined my record buying to second-hand purchases. I had not read any reviews, so the experience was a complete shot in the dark. I was terribly excited. After what I considered to be six spectacular albums, with *Blonde on Blonde* being ground-breaking, I had high expectations.

This new mellow Dylan was not what I had been expecting. I listened through a few times. The simpler style lacked the bite of his previous three electric masterpieces. I searched for the social comment, barbed phrases or poetic complexities, but they were not evident. With few exceptions, these offerings were remarkably straightforward and uncomplicated. This Dylan sounded content and laid-back but with a lot of heavy Old Testament sermonising in a number of the tracks. I did not see anything ground-breaking in the album, all very listenable and pleasant, if at times rather dour.

I contained my disappointment and put it down to circumstance. Bob was getting his feet back in the water. Whilst not brilliant, this was at least a return. It was great to have him back. We'd be getting more further down the line.

'John Wesley Harding' (Bob Dylan)

The opening track set the tone for Dylan's re-entry. While the sixties music scene had exploded into experimentation, lysergically charged psychedelia, heavy metal and jazz-fused progressive rock, full of social and political content - such as The Doors 'Unknown Soldier' and 'The End', Country Joe and the Fish with 'Feel Like I'm Fixing To Die Rag' and 'Untitled Protest' and The Who's 'Won't Get Fooled Again' and the Beatles 'Revolution', Bob had veered off in the other direction. Completely out of sync with the times, he's retreated to his folk roots and Guthrie-esque songs. Gone was the ground-breaking thin, wild mercury sound. Although it was a return to his roots, it was very different. It lacked the raw edge. This 'new' Dylan sounded content. The sound he was producing could best be described as mellow – not a word I would have applied to much of Dylan's output up to now.

The track was very much based on the Woody Guthrie song 'Pretty Boy Floyd', a song about a kind-hearted outlaw. In real life, John Wesley Hardin (no 'g') was a mean outlaw killer who claimed to have killed 42 people – a strange choice of hero for the track. Was the misspelling deliberate? The real John Wesley hurt many a man and was a mean drunken bastard. He made plenty of foolish moves. Bob changed it all into a simple tale of a pleasant, idealised character. Lyrically unchallenging.

The track is acoustically based with a strummed guitar tuned to F major with a capo on the fifth fret, playing a simple C, F and G chord sequence. It has a smooth, warm feel to it. The accompaniment comes in with a great walking bass, some brisk drums and pleasant harmonica to continue the laid-back atmosphere and pared-back production. Even Bob's voice sounds different, smoother and less raspy. He later explained that as having given up smoking.

'As I Went Out One Morning' (Bob Dylan)

I found this the most intriguing track on the album. On the surface, it appeared like another straightforward narrative, except that, intriguingly, it did not make sense. That seemed more like the Dylan of old, even if it was totally lacking in the surreal poetic imagery of past albums.

The music follows the same mood as on the opening track – a smooth, mellowness. It is played in the key of F minor with a capo on the fourth fret. The chords are based around F, C, D and A but the song is led by an outstanding complex bassline with that same brisk drumming and smooth harmonica playing as on 'John Wesley Hardin'. It gives the piece a late-night feel.

The lyrics appear to be based on the W. H. Auden poem 'As I Went Out One Morning'. Bob has adapted it to tell a tale of slavery and betrayal. The peculiar twist is the use of Tom Paine as the slave owner. Tom Paine was the atheist architect of American independence. He wrote *The Rights of Man* and was an antislavery abolitionist. There must have been a reason to use him in this way and the most likely one goes back to Bob's embarrassing accolade of the Tom Paine Award in 1963. A drunken Bob was out of his depth and found the whole award ceremony, with its middle-aged, wealthy benefactors, grotesque. He did not want to be part of it. Apart from the slavery element, there are hints of misogyny and women's liberation but nothing overt. All told a simple lyric that leaves more mystery than clarity but certainly created plenty to wonder at.

'I Dreamed I Saw St. Augustine' (Bob Dylan)

My view is that this is the key to the 'new' Dylan displayed on this album. This song, in the form of a dream, is a clue to what is going on in Bob's head – guilt. Following his motorbike accident, he'd been allowed to reflect and, always having had a penchant for religion – evident in his upbringing – his extensive knowledge of the bible and the occurrence of religious themes in his songs, he was reviewing the past handful of debauched years of his life as sinful. He had rested his head on the glass that separated God from man. Augustine (depending on which one you choose) was a radical, staunch Catholic who believed that sinners, including unbaptised babies, burnt in hell. Bob used him as a convenient prophet of doom. He was racked with regrets and wished to repent. Hence the replacement of the rebellious, hard-living, left-leaning rock star with this clean-living new image and identification with evangelical idols.

The song itself was ironically based on the 'The Ballad of Joe Hill', both lyrically and musically, which had been written in 1936 by Alfred Hayes about the socialist trade union organiser Joe Hill who was wrongly accused of murder and sentenced to death. His last words were 'Don't waste time mourning – Organise!'. Joan Baez had played the song to Bob earlier and often included it in her repertoire.

The music follows the same easy-going style. It's in the key of F major with a capo on the fifth fret. The C, F, D and A chords create a light flowing sound, the backing of throbbing bass and drums sparse and unobtrusive. The song is slower and melancholy in feel, the harmonica mournful, Bob's voice smooth, singing well within himself.

'All Along the Watchtower' (Bob Dylan)
A change of pace to a brighter tune with more impetus and impact. We're no longer in that wee wee hours mode. The guitar is tuned to C minor with a capo on the fourth fret and the chords A, G and F provide a compelling riff that repeats to set up a circular pattern. It drives along straight out of that somnambulant groove into a brighter mode without losing the acoustic background. The drums are brisker, the bass quicker and the harmonica insistent. Those chord changes create momentum and add interest. It is powerful even if it is not progressing anywhere.

The lyrics have shades of the Dylan of old with their jokers, thieves, princes and growling wildcats. We're in a stark landscape back in history populated by mysterious horsemen, howling winds and threatening watchtowers. The song takes the form of a conversation between the joker and the thief – the joker probably being Dylan and the thief Albert Grossman. On one level, it's a portrait of Dylan and his manager in the skulduggery of the music business. On another level, we're back in the religious context with biblical input from the Book of Isaiah, the whole charade of life being a pointless exercise from which there is no escape.

Death is approaching.

This track is the most outstanding on the album, but it was completely overshadowed when Jimi Hendrix got his frets on it and tore it into something else. With Jimi, the wind didn't just howl – it was whipped into a tornado. Bob released his version as a single which went nowhere; Jimi's version shot into the top ten. Even Bob admitted that Jimi's version was definitive and adopted his arrangement in future live performances.

'The Ballad of Frankie Lee and Judas Priest' (Bob Dylan)
Back to simplicity with this Spartan acoustic number. The song is in C major with the capo on the fifth fret. The chords move through an unassuming repeating G, B, A progression, creating a cyclic pattern behind which the bass is busy but back in the mix and the drums quietly plod along. The cycle is only broken by a short harmonica break prior to the last verse.

Bob tells the story of the two protagonists, one offering financial support, the other contemplating what to do. Jesus and the Devil? Bob and the music business? Launching himself into the earthly delights, as portrayed in the bordello, he finds that, far from satisfying his needs, it is killing him. The real reward is not to be found in temptation but in paradise. I think we're back into Bob's newfound revelation. Perhaps the moral of this story is that the music business is not a friendly home and that fortune and fame are not the paradise they seemed to be from afar.

'Drifter's Escape' (Bob Dylan)

This track, performed in the key of A major with a capo on the second fret, is a simple rotating two-chord pattern between G and C. It is reputed to have been written on a train going into New York for the first sessions. The guitar and band certainly chug along as if on a locomotive; even the harmonica has a freight train quality.

Dylan puts himself in the position of a harmless bewildered wanderer cast adrift in a world he doesn't understand, being put through some Kafka-esque trial in which he doesn't know what he's accused of, the crowd baying for his blood, saved by Old Testament divine intervention. Is this the story of Bob's career? The fury he engenders with his musical changes. Was the motorbike accident the divine intervention that saved him from his comeuppance?

'Dear Landlord' (Bob Dylan)

Side two starts with a dour, complex piano blues number. The dirge-like delivery has a complicated chord structure, throwing around multiple chords – C, A, G, F, B and D – to create a sophisticated melody. For me, the result sounds dreary and Bob's voice a melancholy drawl, failing to be lifted by the steady drumbeat and driving bass with its gorgeous repeating refrain.

Dylan claimed that the lyrics were abstract with no target in mind. I'm not so sure. It certainly comes across as a bargaining between Bob and his manager Albert Grossman, who coincidentally just happened to be his landlord at the time. Mind you; it could also be interpreted as Bob down on his knees pleading with his God, which would fit the prevailing mood.

'I Am A Lonesome Hobo' (Bob Dylan)

Despite the dire warning inherent in the track, this song, in the key of G major, has a great jaunty, rockin' rhythm. Even the harmonica sounds chirpy. The acoustic guitar is very much to the fore, setting a superb repeating rhythm behind which the bass and drums do little more than compliment. It makes a contrast to the previous track.

Once again, Bob puts himself in the position of the hobo, the outsider. It's a position he's adopted on many occasions. He likes seeing himself in that role. Only this time, he's using it as a dire warning to us all. He's telling us that he's been a bad guy and it's brought him down: 'I've tried my hand at bribery, blackmail and deceit'. He's saying that he's been corrupted by his life but now he's repenting. That fits in with his recent epiphany and complete change in personality. The reference to the brother that he is supposed to have harmed, I don't personally see in any biblical Cain and Abel setting. I think it's more generalised than that.

This 'letter' ends with a few words of advice for us – 'Stay free from petty jealousy. Live by no man's code, and keep your judgement to yourself lest you wind up on this road.'

'I Pity the Poor Immigrant' (Bob Dylan)

This song is simply depressing. Another bleak Old Testament judgement straight out of Leviticus, steeped in false empathy, judgement and condemnation, deploying a morose stereotypical portrait of immigrants. They are portrayed as miserable, godless, lying, cheating outsiders who put money before everything else.

The self-pitying tone is perpetuated through the music – a plodding pace with squeaky harmonica – the guitar working through chords C, F, G, A and E with the capo on the fifth fret to create a backdrop with few redeeming features. Once again, Bob has 'acquired' the melody from a traditional source – 'Come all ye Tramps and Hawkers' – just like he was prone to doing back in his early days.

Perhaps we should move away from the literal and reinterpret the term 'immigrant'? Could this be Bob, in his new cleaned-up family man guise, referring to himself in his past life as an outsider? Is it about his Jewish heritage and their life as outsiders? If so, it's pretty harsh. Or perhaps, given Bob's new conversion, we should substitute 'disbeliever' for 'immigrant' and place God as the narrator?

'The Wicked Messenger' (Bob Dylan)

Despite being another doom-laden offering straight out of Proverbs, the music, in the key of A major played with a capo on the second fret, is upbeat and moves at a fast pace with much vocal inflection. The ascending bass drives the piece, amusingly reminding me of Nancy Sinatra's *Boots*, with the drums shuffling along and Bob producing some fast acoustic guitar phrases in elegant strumming patterns using the chords G and F. The whole thing begins with the shrillest harmonica intro.

The lyrics are less upbeat. The messenger is sent from God to impart his message but is viewed as wicked, his message not understood and viewed as trivial, so he is ignored and shunned. Hell is at hand as the ground heats up, the leaves fall and the seas part as we approach the end. But the gospel is good news.

'Down Along the Cove' (Bob Dylan)

Phew! A light, breezy piano, twelve-bar country blues number in B major, devoid of any heavy Old Testament overtones. The bass bubbles happily along, the drums have a continuous shuffling beat, there are blues harp flourishes and even a touch of steel guitar to endow it with an easy-going country feel. It sounds a little like Dylan of old but with a lighter, more contented tone.

We're in holiday mode, meeting up, strolling along the beach hand in hand in the sunshine. This is the new family man Dylan, in love, happy and content. It's a pretty little ditty – nothing more.

'I'll Be Your Baby Tonight' (Bob Dylan)

The album ends with a jaunty love song that is very late-night and smoochy. They obviously wanted to leave on a light note after all the heavy sermonising. The harmonica is lazily wistful, the drumming light-touch, the bass slow and easy-going, and the steel guitar creates a nocturnal jazzy feel with country overtones.

Bob and Sara are settling in for an evening of passion. They're shutting out all the criticism and aggro, closing the shutters on the world and grabbing a bottle.

This is precisely where the new Dylan was at.

Nashville Skyline (1969)

Personnel:

Bob Dylan: guitar, harmonica, vocals

Norman Blake: guitar

Kenneth A. Buttrey: drums, bongos, cowbell

Johnny Cash: vocal, guitar on 'Girl From the North Country'

Fred Carter Jr: guitar

Charlie Daniels: guitar, bass

Pete Drake: pedal steel guitar

Marshall Grant: bass on 'Girl From the North Country'

W. S. Holland: drums on 'Girl From the North Country'

Charlie McCoy: guitar, harmonica

Bob Wilson: organ, piano

Bob Wooton: guitar on 'Girl From the North Country'

Elliot Landy: photography

Al Clayton: photography

Bob Johnson: producer

Charlie Bragg: engineer

Neil Wilburn: engineer

Label: Colombia

Recorded at Colombia Studio B Nashville

Release date: April 1969

Highest chart positions: UK: 1 US: 3

It was now 1969 and the United States was in turmoil. The Vietnam War and civil rights movement had polarised the country. Martin Luther King Jr. and senator Robert F. Kennedy, widely seen as the next President, were both assassinated. Woodstock would happen in the Summer. There was huge confrontation in the streets of Chicago at the Democratic Convention in 1968. American cities had burnt in race riots. Bob Dylan had previously been a leading light in voicing the views of the anti-war and civil rights movement. The sixties underground movement had taken on these issues and it had brought them into violent conflict with the establishment. The sixties music was reflecting these issues. This was the background. Despite the innocuous nature of the previous album, there was still great expectation for the next. The hope was that Bob would have found his feet and the music and lyrics would once again reach the musical and poetic standards of previous albums. There was certainly enough grist for the mill.

This was the year that The Beatles brought out *Abbey Road*. They'd already released 'Strawberry Fields Forever' and 'Revolution 1'. Hendrix had released *Electric Ladyland* the year before. Led Zeppelin and Cream were in the charts. Captain Beefheart, The Doors, Jefferson Airplane and Frank Zappa were setting the pace. The Stones were letting it bleed and The Who were telling us about Tommy. Roy Harper was producing a 20-minute epic on

Folkjokeopus. There were tons of sobs with Free and Pink Floyd was giving us more. The MC5 were kicking out the jams and Iggy was stooging. The scene was buzzing with loud noise, energy, politics and confrontation. The underground had become mainstream. revolution was in the air. In the midst of this heavy metal, psychedelic swirl, Bob had reappeared. This was his second foray after his disappearance.

As a 20-year-old student living in London and deeply immersed in the underground scene, I was hoping the new Dylan album would reflect the values of his earlier albums. I bought the album with some trepidation. Bringing the album home, I played it through from beginning to end, took it outside, smashed it and threw it in the bin.

This new, clean-cut, right-wing, unhip, establishment kid playing little country ditties of little consequence could not possibly be the same fire-breathing, cool, hip, snarling, demon poet rebel who had blasted the establishment, the hypocrisy of all its institutions (including religion) and had been the pin-up boy of the underground. We watched this little clean-shaven kid playing his superficial songs at the Isle of Wight Festival and we could not believe it. Where was he?

The Vietnam War was raging. The anti-establishment forces were in open conflict with the authorities. Protest was in full swing. Civil rights, anti-war, social change, women's liberation, environmentalism – the times were truly changing. Where was the architect? What did he have to offer?

By now, we had Webberman going through Dylan's dustbins, claiming this post-accident Dylan was an impostor, then claiming that Dylan was on heroin. He said that the album was 'A sell-out to pig culture'. But was it? Looking back through the decades, would it appear in a different light? No. Not for me.

Early in 1969, Bob went into the studio in Nashville to begin recording the follow-up to *John Wesley Harding*. Instead of the pared-back sound he had used on that album, he had the intention of using a much fuller band vibe. For those of us eager to hear the hard-edged blues of *Highway 61 Revisited* or the more complex wild, thin mercury vibe of *Blonde on Blonde,* we were in for a big disappointment. There was no return to the surreal poetry either. *Nashville Skyline* was simple, bland, pleasant country music. Easy listening and as far from ground-breaking as you could get. I'd go so far as calling it cosy and on a par with Val Doonican. For heaven's sake, it even had the straight redneck Johnny Cash dueting with him. In my top thousand albums, it comes in at three million and seven, just above *Self Portrait.*

Fortunately, it was only ten short tracks long and one of them was an instrumental while another was a reinvention of an early song. He was struggling to come up with enough new material. Mind you, the critics loved it and so did the public. Bob was not in the least contrite:

These are the type of songs that I always felt like writing. The songs reflect more of the inner me than the songs of the past. They're more to my base than, say, *John Wesley Harding*. There I felt like everyone expected me to be a poet, so that's what I tried to be.

Sometimes, in the fullness of time, some 53 years in this case, one can go back and reappraise an album and come up with a different assessment. Without the baggage of youth, the weight of expectation, or the traps of its time, one can hear it in a different light. Not in this case. I hear it exactly the way I heard it 53 years ago. In my opinion, this whole album is vacuous, trivial, frivolous and twee. With ten short tracks, it's also thankfully short.

I'm not sure why it was so short. Bob had been laying down lots of demos at Big Pink (later to come out as *The Basement Tapes*). He had many songs to choose from – many that were superior to this sad bunch.

'Girl From the North Country' (Duet with Johnny Cash) (Bob Dylan)
The album starts with a rendition of the song he had stolen from Martin Carthy's version of 'Scarborough Fair'. He claimed to have written it, but in truth, he had merely adapted the original melody a little and used many of the original words.

This version is a smooth ironed-out facsimile of the original – tidied up with two acoustic guitars, a light rhythm section, and changed into a soft croon. There's no sign of the raw energy of the original that he had dedicated to first love in Hibbing Echo Helstrom.

'Nashville Skyline Rag' (Bob Dylan)
If anybody was in any doubt as to what to expect from the album, this harmless little country workout would put their minds at rest. Bob described it as a bit of fun. This pleasant little tune was constructed around Dylan's 1963 outtake 'Suze (The Cough Song)'. Based around the chords C, F, G, D, E, and A, the band set about producing an instrumental to show off their virtuosity. It starts with a picked guitar and squeaky harmonica, then onto strummed guitar before each band member enters one after another to display their mastery – guitar solos, steel guitar, piano – all very jolly. In all, three minutes of fluff.

'To Be Alone With You' (Bob Dylan)
This happy little ditty is based around the E, A and B chords. It starts with a tinkling piano and strummed guitar as Dylan asked Bob Johnson if the tape is rolling. When he gets the nod, they launch into a conventional country number. It's upbeat, with the bass bobbing about and the piano tinkling Jerry Lee Lewis country style. The electric guitar is subdued and the drums buried, but the band are tight and the track has a nice melody.

Bob's vocal, now that he's free of cigarettes, has become much smoother and less nasal. It suits this new harmless country style – the track being called a sweet song with a pretty melody – and that's what it is – a pleasant love song. He does manage to throw in a little nod to Ray Charles with the R&B lyrics: 'The nighttime is the right time to be with the one you love.' The rest of the lyrics are forgettable.

'I Threw It All Away' (Bob Dylan)
A song that maybe should have been written in the present tense. He's certainly chucking the chords around on this one – A, D, C, E, F and G are all used in this unambiguous song of regret. It could have been written for any number of Bob's past lovers – Echo, Suze, Joan, Nico or Edie. He threw them all away with his incessant cheating. There is a little sexual imagery, but apart from that, the lyrics are straightforward and direct.

The musical presentation is one of sadness expressed through a delicately picked acoustic guitar with an organ providing elongated notes. The drums and bass hold down a platform for the melody, which is soft and remorseful. Bob's newfound voice is smooth and emotional as he croons away.

It was released as a single and rightly only achieved the lower reaches of the charts. It is remarkably unspectacular.

'Peggy Day' (Bob Dylan)
Another track that was trivial and pointless. Based around the chords F, D, G and C, Bob was crooning away over the top of some jazz guitar reminiscent of Django Reinhardt but not anywhere near as exciting. He is in love with Peggy Day – whoever she is and as if we care.

It's another two minutes of my life I'll never get back, but at least it made Bob happy. I was sure by now that I preferred him a lot grumpier.

'Lay Lady Lay' (Bob Dylan)
The track, written in A major and deploying the chords A, C, G, B and F to create an atmospheric melody, is very organ based with an intricate drumbeat tapping a fast rhythm while the organ swirls. The bass is used to emphasise the chords and the guitar only really appears halfway through to embellish the middle section. Bob croons away in a low pitch.

Bob denies that the content is sexual, though I don't know how on earth you could interpret it any other way. It's either sexual anticipation or coercive control.

It was originally written for the film *Midnight Cowboy* but was too late to be considered. Bob later said that it was written for Barbra Streisand, but I think that was just a joke.

Despite many radio stations refusing to play it, the undemanding song was very popular and took Bob back into the top ten.

'One More Night' (Bob Dylan)
A bright, jaunty little country number in the key of C major. There's picked acoustics, strummed acoustics, a steel guitar and a conventional country

backing, even Bob's mellow drawl is country. The track is catchy and danceable. It is so country I thought Bob was taking the piss. This is exactly the kind of music he was criticising in the past: 'the country music station played soft, but there was nothing, really nothing to turn off.'

Even the lyrics are saccharine country. The moon is the satellite of love and is shining on everyone but him. He could not be what she wanted him to be. She's to blame. She could not be true. She's gone and he's in misery. Isn't this a countrified version of 'It Ain't Me Babe'?

'Tell Me That it Isn't True' (Bob Dylan)

Another sweet poppy country ballad based around the chords C, G, and F, using rather twee-strummed guitar patterns. The organ and piano beef up the sound with the organ performing what, to my ears, comes over as bland annoying fills and there's a picked acoustic break. Not much to say about the rhythm section, which is merely standard for the genre. Bob's nicotine-free voice warbles over the top, sounding mellow.

Once again, we're in clichéd country mode of betrayal and infidelity. She's been seen with another guy who is dark and handsome. He's forlornly pleading with her to tell him it isn't true. Bearing in mind that this is from a time when a newlywed Bob was the happy family man, madly in love with Sara his wife and with a child he was doting on and besotted with. It doesn't ring true.

'Country Pie' (Bob Dylan)

There's a lot of chord variation in this fun up-tempo country romp. He fiddles around with A, D, F, B and E to create a vacuous jolly interval – nothing more. Even if the pie is, as has been suggested, some sexual metaphor, it still does little to arouse my interest in this jingle.

'Tonight I'll Be Staying Here With You' (Bob Dylan)

The album ends with this lightweight epitaph of a contented man. The piano-based standard country song, built around the chords G, C, B and A, is nothing out of the ordinary, with its mundane backing and wafting steel guitar, except that it chucks in a couple of extra bars to keep the musicians and audience on their toes.

He's changed his mind. He's decided not to go away after all. He's staying home with you. Is this Bob reaffirming to Sara that he's giving up his career, his gruelling life on the road, to stay home with her and the kids? Frankly, I'm past caring.

Self Portrait (1970)

Personnel:
Bob Dylan: guitar, harmonica, keyboards, vocals, cover artwork
Byron Bach: cello
Brenton Banks: violin
George Binkley III: violin
Norman Blake: guitar
David Bromberg: guitar, dobro, bass guitar
Albert Wynn Butler: clarinet, saxophone
Kenneth A. Buttrey: drums, percussion
Fred Carter Jr.: guitar
Marvin Chantry: viola
Ron Cornelius: guitar
Charlie Daniels: bass guitar, guitar
Rick Danko: bass guitar, vocals
Pete Drake: steel guitar
Delores Edgin: vocals
Fred Foster: guitar
Solie Fott: violin, viola
Bubba Fowler: guitar
Dennis Good: trombone
Emanuel Green: violin
Hilda Harris: vocals
Levon Helm: mandolin, drums, vocals
Freddie Hill: trumpet
Karl Himmel: clarinet, saxophone, trombone
Garth Hudson: keyboards
Lilian Hunt: violin
Bob Johnston: production
Martin Katahn: violin
Doug Kershaw: violin
Al Kooper: guitar, horn, keyboards
Sheldon Kurland: violin
Richard Manuel: piano, vocals
Martha McCrory: cello
Charlie McCoy: guitar, bass guitar, harmonica, vibes
Barry McDonald: violin
Tony Terran: trumpet
Ollie Mitchell: trumpet
Carol Montgomery: vocals
Bob Moore: bass guitar
Gene A. Mullins: baritone horn
Joe Osborn: guitar, bass guitar
June Page: vocals

Rex Peer: trombone
Bill Pursell: piano
Robbie Robertson: guitar, vocals
Albertine Robinson: vocals
Al Rogers: drums
Frank Smith: trombone
Maretha Stewart: vocals
Gary Van Osdale: viola
Bill Walker: arrangements
Bob Wilson: organ, piano
Stu Woods: bass guitar
Bob Johnson: producer
Label: Colombia
Recorded at Columbia B studios Nashville
Release date: June 1970
Highest chart positions: UK: 1 US: 3

Bob had opted out. It was as simple as that. There was speculation at the time that he was merely fulfilling a contractual obligation, but it was much more than that. He was making a statement. He actively wanted to distance himself from what was going on. He was angry. He wanted to put pay to the whole concept of him being a poet and spokesman for this generation. They were people who he could no longer relate to. They hung around outside his house, climbed on the roof, even broke in. He was scared for his own safety and that of his wife and children. In the end, he had to move back to New York in order to get some privacy:

> There'd be crowds outside my house. And I said, well, fuck it. I wish these people would just forget about me. I wanna do something they can't possibly like; they can't relate to. They'll see it, and they'll listen, and they'll say, 'Well, let's go on to the next person. He ain't sayin' it no more. He ain't givin' us what we want,' you know? They'll go on to somebody else.

In *Chronicles*, Bob talks of how Dostoyevsky had to write stories in order to ward off his creditors 'Just like in the early 70s I wrote albums to ward off mine.'

As for the album, it wasn't so much an album as a bunch of tracks – a few of which were surprisingly good. Over his time in Nashville, Bob had accumulated much detritus. At the start of his recording sessions, the various bands of musicians would warm up by playing something they all knew. Often that was old traditional material, pop songs or even Bob's old songs. He simply scooped it all off the shelf and dumped it together. There was enough to make a double album:

I'd also seen that I was representing all these things that I didn't know anything about. It was all storming the embassy type of stuff – Abbie Hoffman in the streets – and they sorta figured I was the kingpin of all that. I said, 'Wait a minute, I'm just a musician. So my songs are about this and that. So what?' But people need a leader. People need a leader more than a leader needs people, really. I didn't want that, though.

The album was intended to be dire and get a lot of people off his back. Ironically, despite eliciting terrible reviews, the album sold and was a commercial success. It seems that a lot of people liked unchallenging material. Not only that, but it failed miserably at getting people off his back, succeeding only in getting Webberman to go through his dustbins all the more and reinvigorate his claims of this Dylan being an impostor. Even the cover was a joke. Bob had dashed off a painting in five seconds flat and called the album *Self Portrait*, suggesting that this was a portrait of what he was really like.

This withdrawal asks important questions: who was this person called Bob Dylan? Did he ever really believe those things he was singing and saying in his previous incarnations? Was he an opportunist who had jumped on trend after trend, attempting to be popular? Was he a chameleon who changed his spots according to who he'd been hanging out with? Regarding Bob and his career, these are still pertinent.

These warm-up songs were a right old mixture of old traditional folk songs, pop songs, instrumentals, the odd blues song, plus a few covers of his own material. Because the recordings were from Nashville and spread over a period of time, there was a multitude of musicians and a range of styles. The only thing that holds it together was the lack of gravity of the recordings. These were warm-up tracks never intended for release.

So why was it a double album? 'Well, it wouldn't have held up as a single album – then it really would have been bad, you know. I mean, if you're gonna put a lot of crap on it, you might as well load it up.'

'All the Tired Horses' (Bob Dylan)
Well, as Bob said, they are warm up songs, never intended for release. This is Bob's backing singers, Hilda Harris, Albertine Robinson, and Maeretha Stewart, warming up in the studio by singing a couple of lines of Bob's words in the key of C. They repeat the line a large number of times, adding an 'mmm' at the end. First, it's acapella before a little instrumentation features and then they've plastered it with schmaltzy strings. They harmonise beautifully for three minutes and eleven seconds but…'mmm'. This goes nowhere and no sight of Dylan. Was this an intended girl chorus for a song that never got recorded?

'Alberta #1' (Traditional)
This is a traditional blues song often played by Leadbelly. It dates way back to the early nineteenth century. My favourite version is by Snooks Eaglin. He

adds a little New Orleans flavour to it. Bob's version is excellent. It may be a warm-up, but the relaxed atmosphere and slow pace add to the intimacy. It's an acoustic guitar jam with a bass pattern that moves it along. As well as the inclusion of some harmonica, a female chorus features at the end. The languid mood really suits it. I can imagine the guys all sitting around limbering up in the studio before embarking on a recording session. It works. Great version.

'I Forgot More Than You'll Ever Know' (Cecil A. Null)
After the sublime, we're back to the terrible with this schmaltzy, saccharine country song. It's played with the chords G, C and D, complete with a female chorus, plodding beat, predictable guitars and clichéd steel guitar. Bob's voice crooning over the top is embarrassing. Even the lyrics are a country cliché. The man is telling the man now dating his ex that he knows more about her than he'll ever know. It's heading for a showdown. A track with no redeeming flaws.

'Days of 49' (A Lomax, J Lomax, Frank Warner)
The song goes right back to a poem written by Joaquin Miller about the gold rush of 1849. It was adapted into a song with a chorus added by Charles Bensell in 1872, first published in 1884. John and Alan Lomax, archivists of traditional folk music, were given the song in 1941.

The song tells the story of the lawless gold prospecting days of the great 1849 gold rush – a riotous tale of drunkenness, gambling, fights and death as told by a lone surviving old timer, one old Tom Moore, reminiscing about the past. It's an action-packed tale told through a number of verses.

The song, based around the chords A, G, C and F, sounds very well-rehearsed. If this is thrown together, it certainly shows the quality of the musicians. The guitars gel together and the rhythm section is brilliant. The piano fits in snugly. It's a great platform for Bob to recount the story, which he does with aplomb, his voice in great shape. It has a catchy chorus too!

'Early Mornin' Rain' (Gordon Lightfoot)
Gordon Lightfoot is a 'nice' contemporary singer-songwriter who, like John Denver, wrote some very pleasant tunes – perhaps a little too lightweight and mainstream. This is probably Lightfoot's best track and has a beautifully delicate melody that Bob does justice to even if it is mawkish.

The song is built around the C, G and D chords. It starts with plucked guitars laying down the bedrock whilst the harmonica takes on the melody before the piano takes over while the gentle drumming forms the backdrop. Bob's new voice works with this kind of gentle ballad and it's only towards the end that you get the feeling that it's a warm-up take.

'In Search of Little Sadie' (Traditional)
Now, this does sound like what it is: Bob and the musicians messing about in the studio. He has taken an old blues number dating back to 1922 and is

playing about with both the chords and tempo, which is why it sounds so 'stop and start'. He's thrown in a whole bunch of chords – G, A, B, F, D, C and E – often in unusual arrangements. It sounds as if the band is desperately trying to follow Dylan's lead and find some footing. The song is in the 'Hey Joe' mould in that it is about a guy who shot his woman dead and is then brought to justice. There are many versions under a variety of different names. The result may sound slapdash but it is strangely compulsive. I would like to have heard this recorded properly with a hard blues sound.

'Let it Be Me' (Gilbert Becaud, Mann Curtis, Pierre Delanoe)
This is the lilting Everly Brothers classic from the fifties. It was originally a French song called 'Je T'Appartiens' and was a minor hit in France before being translated to English; The Everly's bring its saccharine lyrics and delicate melody to life with their gorgeous harmonies. Not so, Bob. His new voice does lend itself to a smooth and delicate sensibility and the track has a lot of beauty in it. However, despite the tight backing band and the powerful wail of the female chorus, it is simply the wrong material. Far too lightweight and Bob cannot get near the perfection of Don and Phil's flawless blend.

I can see why they used it as a warm-up track, though – it is a great song and uses a lot of chords. Good for limbering up the musicians on a track that they'd all be familiar with.

'Little Sadie' (Traditional)
Another outing for 'Little Sadie'. This is a different arrangement of the earlier 'In Search Of Little Sadie', but it's the same song.

The earlier track was slower and more bluesy but this version canters along. It's an acoustic guitar battle with the drums setting up a clattering pace. Bob's changed the whole vibe and created something completely different. This is far more country. There isn't the array of experimental chords or any of the stop-start tempo changes. The ending shows what it is – a studio warm-up track. Good though.

'Woogie Boogie' (Bob Dylan)
A little slab of vintage fifties boogie-woogie rockabilly based around some great guitar riffs, boogie-woogie piano and even a wailing sax. The band is having fun on this instrumental. Not sure where Bob is.

'Belle Isle' (Traditional)
This is a lesson in how to ruin a perfectly good song. The answer is to use a very pedestrian backing, a pop arrangement and douse it in really cheesy strings.

This is an old traditional song that tells the story of Cupid and Psyche. If Bob had done it with just the guitars, which can be heard picking away, and not used that naff voice, it would have been excellent.

'Living the Blues' (Bob Dylan)

A standard country song in the key of C. There is a definite nod to 'Singing the Blues' written by Melvin Endsley and recorded by Guy Mitchell. It is sung in the conventional manner. Indeed, everything about the song, from its chord progression to its middle eight, screams the conventional. This is little more than a rather trite country ballad with nothing exceptional in the backing, arrangement, structure, content or delivery. His woman's left him. It's terrible.

'Like a Rolling Stone' (Bob Dylan)

This is the recording of the live performance at the Isle of Wight Festival in which Bob performs a different arrangement of this masterpiece. The live performance, littered with faults, is a lacklustre performance of a brilliant song. It's important as a historical recording but if I want to listen to the song I'll go for the original. If I wanted a live version, I'd choose the raw, jagged version delivered in Newport in 1965. This version is OK.

'Copper Kettle' (Albert Frank Beddoe)

This is an old traditional song that he would have heard Joan Baez perform. It tells the story of a tax-evading moonshiner making whiskey. It's a great song though I'm not so keen on this commercial arrangement. With Bob's new smooth voice, the cheesy strings and the female chorus pinging away in the background, they've turned it into a pop song. In my opinion, this sanitised production has reduced a great song down to a saccharine, sweet parody.

They probably put all that frippery on the track because they put it out as the B-side of the only single from the album.

'Gotta Travel On' (Paul Clayton, Larry Ehrlich, David Lazar, Tom Six)

This song is a fast-paced country song with a rock edge. The chords A, D and C are used to create a driving, freight-train sound. The band is tight and captures the sway of the train with some superb drumming. In this instance, the female chorus adds to the composition. Bob's vocal is good on this track as he is not singing in that angelic sugar-sweet tone that he seems to have adopted for these country-style sessions.

The song itself was credited to Paul Clayton but dates back to at least 1927. Bill Monroe produced a great version in 1957, but Bob most probably got it from Pete Seeger. It tells the simple story of someone who has stayed away from home too long and is catching a train to go back.

'Blue Moon' (Lorenz Hart, Richard Rodgers)

An early Rodgers and Hart number from 1934 that became a standard. Elvis did a great rock version in 1956 and the doo-wop band The Marcels had a massive hit with it in 1961. After that, everyone in the world did a cover version, but

I still never expected to hear Bob do one. It's a revelation. He's turned rock and doo-wop into pop. His smooth voice, so unlike Dylan, handles the melody well with the female chorus oooing and a light conventional backing tinkling away. They've splashed sax over it and then violin. The whole thing sounds highly commercial – can this still be Dylan? While Hendrix was ripping up the US anthem with shrieking feedback, The Beatles were strawberrying the fields and the MC5 were kicking out the jams, Bob was crooning. It feels a lot like Beethoven playing The Monkees. I can't get my head around it.

'The Boxer' (Paul Simon)
Well, it's a folk song of sorts – a commercialised version – and one of Simon and Garfunkel's greatest hits; a marketable number with a lilting melody and quite a hook. No wonder it was a hit. But what was Bob doing covering numbers like this? It is just too 'nice'. The Dylan of a couple of years ago would have sneered at it. Not only that but how on earth could Dylan hope to compete with the sophistication of the Simon and Garfunkel harmonising or the massive production that was applied to their commercial offerings?

He had a go at it, harmonising with himself in two different voices. The result was far from silky smooth and more than a little ramshackle. The song is structured around an acoustic strum of the chords C, A, G and F with a low-key nondescript rhythm section and the odd electric twang (and I do mean odd). I would describe the end result as 'interesting', pleasant, utterly lightweight and disturbing. Bob Dylan doing pop? It's like the sixties never happened. It's like Bob Dylan never happened.

'The Mighty Quinn (Quinn The Eskimo)' (Bob Dylan)
An original, at that point unreleased song, by Bob. A version was on *The Basement Tapes,* but that wasn't going to be officially released for another year or two. The version here is the chaotic live one from the Isle of Wight festival – a plodding chaotic outing. The band sounds very disjointed, plodding along as if they are struggling to keep up. The guitar is fluffed and the chorus responses are distant. Sounds like Dylan singing with a pub band. Strange, because it's a simple enough song. The verse is basically chords C and F, moving to C, G, F and C in the chorus. Perhaps they didn't rehearse enough? They sound like they're having a good time, though.

Dylan described the song as a nursery rhyme. Quinn, the new Messiah, the Eskimo, arrives on the scene to put an end to all the misery, chaos and despair. He dispenses joy and everybody flocks to him. The character was created from Anthony Quinn's role as an Eskimo in the 1960 film *The Savage Innocents*. What are we meant to construe from these lyrics? Is this Bob being biblical and referring to the end of the world? Or is it Bob comically mocking himself and how he was perceived by many as a new Messiah? Probably just a fun knockabout that, ironically, Manfred Mann covered and took to number one in the charts. Goes to show. A catchy chorus can go a long way.

'Take Me As I Am (Or Let Me Go)' (Boudleaux Bryant)

Bob crooning another utterly forgettable country ballad that is pretty gruesome. Everything, from the noisome steel guitar, the girlie chorus, the plodding bass-driven rhythm and the tinkling piano to the tedious love story is a cliché. Contrived and not nice!

Bordleaux Bryant wrote this. He and his wife Felice wrote a lot of songs that the Everly Brothers used and had big hits with. This wasn't one. This was recorded by 'Little' Jimmy Dickens in 1954.

'Take a Message to Mary' (Felice Bryant, Boudleaux Bryant)

Speak of the Devil! Here is one of Felice and Bordeaux's pop outings for The Everly Brothers, a top 20 hit in 1959. They included some great harmonies which are missing on this version. The tale of this murdering highwayman, who is locked up forever and trying to get a message to his girlfriend to tell her that he's gone away, is musically simplified. It starts with a corny introduction from the girls; then some strummed acoustic before the electric guitar appears – which is more purposeful. At least the band sounds more alive, the drums have some life, the piano tinkles with decisiveness and that guitarist sounds like he means it. Fortunately, the steel guitar doesn't feature much. Bob sings it straight and melodic. The varied A, D, G and C, G, F, C chords are all there.

Is this what we've come to in 1969? Bob Dylan doing covers of sweet fifties pop songs?

'It Hurts Me Too' (Traditional)

This happens to be one of my favourite Elmore James numbers. Before I heard this, I was wondering how Bob, with a bunch of Nashville country musicians, might tackle a hard-edged Chicago blues number. He didn't. He modelled it more on a version of the forties Tampa Red acoustic number. A blues number that went back a lot further than that. Nonetheless, Bob does a great job on it, slowing the track right down to create an authentic bluesy feel. He sounds more like himself here, with a voice full of anguish.

The piece is in the key of C major and centres around two acoustic guitars, with chords C, F and A – one strummed and the other expertly picked. The interaction is brilliant. An upright bass sympathetically provides the accompaniment with sparse thumping notes. The result is an atmospheric blues that, for me, is the standout track on the album.

'Minstrel Boy' (Bob Dylan)

It's another original Dylan composition. We're back to the Isle of Wight festival and a loose, chaotic performance. There are a number of chords – C, F, G and E – and a change of tempo for the chorus. The number starts with a pretty messy bit of acapella. I'm not sure that they can hear each other through the monitors. It's ragged. Following the opening chorus, it eases into a gentle, laid-back rolling number with a nice guitar burst.

It's a strange one and certainly one of Bob's minor compositions. It's telling us that it's been a hard journey getting to the top of the hill in the rock business, but he's got nowhere to go other than forward. He's been lucky, but even after all these love affairs, he's still lonely (I wonder where Sara is in all this – doesn't sound like the contented family husband here). He tells us he's been overworked and mocked, but he's still going. He still doesn't know where the next dollar is coming from.

'She Belongs to Me' (Bob Dylan)
A good sped-up version of the Bob Dylan classic performed at the Isle of Wight festival. The band sound united on this one, with some taut drumming and a superb guitar break. Bob's voice is in good shape, but it becomes so fast that towards the end, he turns it into a kind of jolly with shades of 'Rainy Day Women', which doesn't really suit the seriousness of the content. Although injecting a different musical flavour can be refreshing, I feel that it still needs to be sympathetic to the sentiments. The crowd response is ecstatic, though – perhaps that filled him with adrenalin?

'Wigwam' (Bob Dylan)
It's difficult to know what to make of this instrumental mariachi number, complete with brass. Sounds like the band was having a bit of a laugh with the chords C, F and G, trying to squeeze out a peculiar Mexican sound. It starts with a strange, underlying, growling bass before the band kick in with this wordless happy-go-lucky piece. Bob is first De La-ing, then Pa Da-ing , La de da-ing, Ta la-ing, singing the melody. For a man famous for his words, producer of such poetic, wordy masterpieces as 'Chimes of Freedom', 'It's Alright Ma, I'm Only Bleeding' and 'Gates of Eden' it's a strange place to have arrived at.

Bob released this as a single (with 'Copper Kettle' on the B-side), which was quite successful. What does that tell us? That the public are none too discerning of quality?

'Alberta #2' (Traditional)
The arrangement for this version of *Alberta* renders it a totally different song to the first. Whereas that one was slow and poignant, this one is energetic. The band feels more rehearsed. There's a very steady beat with a lot more harmonica and a female chorus. It has pace, despite the fuller backing, there is a lighter feel, but, for me, it's lost that relaxed atmosphere – it's great, but I favour the first version.

Interestingly, I prefer this album to *Nashville Skyline*. It's occasionally raw and has a lot of corny crap, but there are a small number of tracks that stand out. However, it was just completely out of kilter with what was going on at the time and the whole album is lacking in serious content. The fact that an album of such lightweight material should sell better than albums of sheer quality and genius tells us something about the pop music market. What sells is material that is short, shallow, catchy and sentimental. Music with depth and challenge has a smaller market. Bob, perhaps inadvertently, served that up in spades. He's always told us he's just a song-and-dance man. Now he was demonstrating it.

It's a mishmash of stuff from over two years that was never intended to see the light of day. I hated it when it came out. It was not what I was expecting or wanting from Dylan. I can now appreciate some of the material, even though it's not the Dylan I want. The album makes me sad. It sounds like someone has taken a whole bunch of warm-ups and abandoned oddments from the studio and messed around with them, adding grotesque strings and tarting them about. Shame. This could have been something (after quality control). There's a decent single album in there, even if it's not the Dylan album I was hoping for. I was hoping for something much more challenging. It was going to take a while to get that Dylan back. I wonder what Dylan made of this unexpected success with material that was, whatever way you look at it, substandard?

New Morning (1970)

Personnel:
Bob Dylan: acoustic guitar, electric guitar, harmonica, keyboards, vocals
David Bromberg: electric guitar, dobro
Harvey Brooks: bass
Charlie Daniels: bass
Ron Cornelius: electric guitar
Buzz Feiten: electric guitar
Al Kooper: organ, piano, electric guitar, French horn
Russ Kunkel: drums
Billy Mundi: drums
Hilda Harris: backing vocals
Albertin Robinson: backing vocals
Maeretha Stewart: backing vocals on 'If Dogs Run Free'
Len Siegler: photography
Bob Johnson: producer
Label: Colombia
Recorded at Columbia B and E studios New York
Release date: October 1970
Highest chart positions: UK: 1 US: 7

New Morning shed a glimmer of hope. Following a trio of albums that varied between average and dismal, there was a shred of a rekindling. By now, we knew we were never going to get the old Dylan back. We had to settle for something new. *New Morning* was almost on par with *John Wesley Harding*. Was this now the best that the post-accident Dylan could come up with? Had the mercurial, word-spitting scourge of the establishment, anti-war and civil rights poet, become a died-in-the-wool redneck of limited ability?

In 1971, A.J. Weberman ran the Dylan Liberation Front and continued claiming that Dylan was a sell-out and an imposter. He rummaged through his garbage to find the evidence and claimed to have had interviews and telephone conversations with Bob in which he cajoled him, telling him that he had become a conservative reactionary who just hoarded his money and hung around with ultraconservatives like Johnny Cash. He castigated Dylan for being someone who had ripped off black musicians and culture but now refused to use his money or influence to help any of the poor people that he had so espoused in the past. He'd become a traitor who would not even do benefits in aid of people in dire straits. Was he right? Where was this heroic poet who had done so much to raise peoples' sensitivities? Who had stood up for the poor and downtrodden? Had Dylan simply been subverted by wealth and become one of the capitalists he had so despised?

I saw Joan Baez in the summer of 1971 in Boston. She pleaded from the stage for Bob to come out of hiding and get back into the fray. There was a revolution going on – we desperately needed the old Dylan. But that old Dylan had gone. What we had was *New Morning*.

Work had begun on *New Morning* while they were chucking *Self Portrait* together. Part of it came out of a musical play by the poet Archibald MacLeish called *Scratch*, a version of *The Devil and Daniel Webster*, which Bob had reluctantly been coerced into contributing to. He produced three numbers for the play, including 'New Morning', 'Time Passes Slowly' and 'Father of Night'. The two poets, from very different ages and backgrounds, initially got on very well but later got into a dispute over the lyrics of 'Father of Night'. Bob had written 'Father of day, Father of night/Father of black, Father of white.' Macleish wanted it changed to 'Father of Night, Father of dread/Father of cold in the void overhead/ Father of serpent under the stone/Father of fear in the dark alone.' Bob did not appreciate anyone messing with his lyrics and left the project. The three songs he had written formed the basis of *New Morning*.

A previous session involving George Harrison had produced a number of tracks, including 'If Not For You', but had been scrapped. It did provide some motivation and a song or two to work on for the album. It seemed that the thirst was coming back, though the creative juices were not flowing as sweetly as they had been before. At least some reasonable songs were coming out of his pen and *New Morning* provided a new base to work from.

'If Not For You' (Bob Dylan)

The opener is a sentimental love song with a really catchy melody based around a whole host of complicated chords. Bob has lost that annoying country crooning voice and is back to his more familiar nasally drawl. Excellent.

There is no surreal poetry, obscure meanings, abstract imagery or any such thing – just a straightforward thanks to Sara for all she'd done to heal him. It's a very busy track with a multitude of instruments. Personally, I prefer George Harrison's version with the slide guitar very much to the fore. George turns it into something more spiritual.

Though it is remarkably simple lyrically and is really little more than a solid pop song, I reckon we're off to a good start.

Bob tried it out in the George Harrison session and George included a great version on his first solo outing – the triple album *All Things Must Pass*. The two of them performed this at George's concert for Bangladesh in 1971 (a concert that was instrumental in bringing Bob back to the stage).

The track was released as a single but sadly went nowhere.

'Day of the Locusts' (Bob Dylan)

A piano song that tells the story of how a reluctant Bob Dylan went to pick up his honorary degree from Princetown University in 1970. Honorary degrees are awarded to acknowledge great accomplishment. Bob obviously deserved the recognition, but those hallowed halls of academia represented everything he despised about the establishment. He found it hard to reconcile his anti-establishment stance with recognition from that establishment, looking at it as a gloomy lifeless place of judgement that he likened to a tomb: 'I glanced into the chamber where the judges were talking. Darkness was everywhere, it smelled like a tomb.' He had to be heavily persuaded to go and accept the honour by his wife Sara and David Crosby. Once there, a very stoned Dylan had to be further persuaded to put on the cap and gown.

The ceremony took place just prior to the release of *Self Portrait*. At the ceremony, Bob, already paranoid due to everybody staring at him, was appalled to hear the Chancellor introduce him as 'a spokesman for his generation' and 'the disturbed conscience of young America' – the very things he was trying so hard to escape. It filled him with horror. In his biography, Bob asserts that the line 'The man standin' next to me, his head was exploding. Well, I was prayin' the pieces wouldn't fall on me' referred to his shock at hearing what the man was saying, though David Crosby thought it referred to him and how incredibly stoned he was.

The title of the song is the name of a novel by Nathaneal West, whose theme was the cynical use of the 'American Dream' to exploit people. The establishment waved this idea that anybody could rise to the top; all it took was hard work, when in fact it was bullshit. Bob felt that by accepting the degree he was bolstering this system.

The year he received the degree was indeed the year of the cicada. They come out of the ground every seven years to mate. The sound of their mass stridulations form an ocean of sound. Cicadas are not locusts – but close enough. They represented the natural world outside, full of life and freedom, the opposite of everything turgid within the halls of the establishment.

As for the music, it was a great, melodic piece, a good rock song. Bob starts it off singing with just the piano. The full band comes in at the chorus. It's a very busy sound with lots going on. The percussion is intricate and the bass sets up a heavy beat for the piano to lay down its chords against, while the organ fills out the sound.

'Time Passes Slowly' (Bob Dylan)

One of the numbers that came out of the attempted theatrical collaboration with Archibald MacLeish. On the surface, a slow, dreamy piano tune which captures the mood of the time he was in – out of the limelight, away from the hustle and bustle, free from the pressure. Bob seems to place the piece in the past with reference to wagons – a kind of rural idyll. Yet is everything as idyllic as it sounds? The fact that time is passing slowly indicates boredom. Is Bob beginning to miss being in the centre of things? The music would indicate that.

The song is in the key of E and runs through the D, C, G, E and F chord shapes with the capo. Then, strangely, the instrumental break gets very hectic and aggressive with some stinging guitar. The elements of unrest are present in the arrangement. While the track has an intimate, relaxing feel, it is stained with dissatisfaction.

'Went to See the Gypsy' (Bob Dylan)

The Gypsy is Elvis, a mystical figure, and this song relates to what is probably a genuine experience of Bob going to see Elvis but bottling out at the last minute: 'two or three times we were up in Hollywood, and he had sent some of the Memphis Mafia down to where we were to bring us up to see Elvis. But none of us went'. In the song, Bob is imagining how the meeting might have gone.

Elvis, and the advent of rock 'n' roll, had an enormous impact on Bob back in the fifties but by the late sixties, Elvis was a pop star and a parody of himself. The lyrics indicate that Bob was experiencing a mixture of emotions, daunted at the prospect of meeting with someone he idolised and yet not wanting to see his idol as he was then – not the lean hungry rockabilly hipster of the fifties. He started to go up to see him but decided against it, before a voice in his head (written as a girl calling to him) said 'He did it in Las Vegas, and he can do it here', indicating that he probably still had the magic. Having gathered his courage, he went back but Elvis had left the building. He never did get to see him. The last verse has him looking out from his youth in that little town of Hibbing towards the dream of rock 'n' roll, which young hepcat Elvis represented.

The music is good too – starting with the rhythmic, lightly struck piano repeating the chords G and A, setting the pace and settling into a steady tempo. There is some great pronounced drumming which combines with bass and rhythm guitar to set up a sprightly cadence. The light jazzy organ with its recurring refrain adds body and Bob's vocal is pitched high, clear and full of inflexion. The rhythm guitar asserts itself towards the end with a flurry of notes in the outro. It really works.

'Winterlude' (Bob Dylan)

Sounds like there's a little tension within the Zimmerman household. Calling Sara Winterlude suggests something frosty. Bob wants to put it aside, stop the quarrelling and rectify things with a romantic evening in. A picture of rustic bliss, log fires and snuggling up is painted.

The Winterlude moniker appears to be a made-up word – winter and interlude being combined – indicating a brief thawing in an awkward icy spat. There is a Winterlude festival in Canada, but that didn't start up until many years after Dylan wrote this. They might even have named it after the song.

The song is basically a three-chord pop song with a distinctive Spanish feel (maybe based on a Mexican tune Bob had heard?). A sentimental love song which is really very slushy. It's a waltz with a great memorable melody, a contented, relaxed piece. Harmless enough.

'If Dogs Run Free' (Bob Dylan)

A complete change of direction and atmosphere as Bob ventures into the world of fifties jazz. This poem is put to music and sounds very much like Jack Kerouac's jazz poetry albums. It's in the key of G, founded around a bass progression. The tinkly jazz piano is supplied by Al Kooper and the scat singing by his backing singer Maeretha Stewart. There's some acoustic guitar picking while the drums shuffle lightly with brushes creating that smoky, late-night jazz feel.

The jazz feel is an extension of the poetry with its suggestions of freedom. There's the allusion to the idealised free life of a hobo on the freights without cares or worries. Life could be wondrous. This is pure Kerouac *On the Road* or *Dharma Bums*, or perhaps Guthrie's hobo life. Bob desires to be free from all the trappings of civilisation, free to roam the plains like the cowboys, the Native American Indians and the wildlife. If dogs can do it then why not us?

'New Morning' (Bob Dylan)

It's a new morning. Can't you feel it? Can't you hear it? This is Bob's clarion call. He's declaring a new start! It's the first track on the second side and the album's named after it. On the surface, we have another love song. A contented, nay deliriously happy Bob is driving through the countryside with the one he loves, gorging on the world, basking in the sun, in love and invigorated. But it's more than that – it's a rebirth. He's announcing that he's back on the scene.

The exuberant music announces it too. Starting off with a chugging acoustic, followed by a picked acoustic, the band comes in bouncing along, full of energy. The rotating chords A and D give rise to all manner of chords driving through a host of unusual sequences. It rocks! The organ is happy. The guitar bubbles. Following a slower wistful verse, it's back to the joyful bounce. Can't you feel it? It's called happiness. Everything about it is upward. Bob's alive, in love and everything is alright with the world. He might not be the same Bob we knew on all those sixties albums, but this is the end of the sixties, the start of a new decade and Bob is back.

'Sign on the Window' (Bob Dylan)

We're brought down to earth with a thump. This is the prequel to 'New Morning'. He's alone, miserable, lost and bereft. He's reflecting on a love who has run off with another, feeling as low as he can be. The slow-paced music, in the key of F major, reflects the poignancy. Bob's piano playing is at its most idiosyncratic. The pared-back keyboard captures the low feeling, the yearning and anguish. The solo playing is bleak. The band, with female chorus, comes in between verses and is sympathetic to the mood.

The poet is at work with some clever wordplay, rhyming Main Street with both rain and sleet! I suggest it's the prequel because the last verse, with its wistful dreaming about a future life, surmises that marriage and raising a family make up the most important things in life. That's what it's about. He's come to realise it. It's what he had in 'New Morning'.

'One More Weekend' (Bob Dylan)
Bang! We've launched straight into a boisterous twelve-bar blues in A major with a riff that is reminiscent of those great blues riffs on *Highway 61*. We're in boisterous mood. Drop the kids off, we're heading off for a filthy weekend. Come on honey, take a ride on his deck! He'll make the ocean move. It's full of sexual innuendo with the comin' and goin' of rabbits.

The music is rockin', starting with a reference to Little Richard's 'Slippin' and Slidin''. The rhythm section sets up a dirty blues. That slide guitar continues the theme with some great barrelhouse piano. This rocks like we haven't heard Bob do for years. Classic!

'The Man in Me' (Bob Dylan)
Another piano song in Ab major constructed around the black notes to create a solid country-flavoured soft rock song – Dylan's voice in fine fettle, the female chorus supplying support and that organ augmenting the chorus. I could do without the La-las, which I suppose are intended to create the feel of contentment.

Another tale of rural bliss in which Bob acknowledges the support and importance of his lady. She brings out the best in him. Within this bucolic setting, Bob is content and self-contained, apart from the world and doing his own thing. His woman stands by him and keeps him grounded, encouraging him to open up and express himself. As the chorus suggests, he's in love and it feels good. He has no desire to be part of the machine out there. The world intrudes and closes him off. It takes a special woman to bring him out of himself.

'Three Angels' (Bob Dylan)
This is a strange one – Bob reciting a poem/description of the scene in a small American town around Christmas time. Three angels playing horns up above, as part of a Christmas street decoration, are totally ignored by the various passers-by. Nobody pays them any heed or questions what they are doing. Nobody cares. They probably care even less after this. It's all recited over a cheesy backing that terminates in the most excruciating angelic chorus.

'Father of Night' (Bob Dylan)
Like nothing he has done – a dramatic piano number spraying around the chords C, B, A, G and E on those beloved black keys. It was the main song that Bob wrote for his collaboration with Archibald MacLeish. I think it would have worked very well on stage. It has a compelling tune that constantly drives forward. The oooing female chorus in the background creates a religious, hymnal feel.

It's a very short piece, just over a minute, and I think Bob probably wanted to end the album with it because of both its power and the fact that it is basically a prayer. It has been said to be Bob's interpretation of the Jewish prayer Amidah (meaning standing), which is a central prayer to many Jewish ceremonies. It might have been a vague inspiration, but this is no reworking of that prayer. This number is a simple prayer to God who, according to Bob, has created everything. Bob deploys some simple poetic rhymes to list God's varied creations.

Personally, as a devout atheist, I could have done without these heavy religious sentiments; they rather spoilt the last two tracks of the album for me, though I do appreciate the experimentation and adventure. That's good to see.

Unreleased tracks
'Wallflower'
This track appeared on the *Bootleg Series 1-3*. It was recorded in November 1971 and is an upbeat country song with a danceable beat. The tambourine bashes out the rhythm while the bass thumps along, a steel guitar trills away and Bob puts on his country twang following the melody on the harmonica.

Somehow I can't imagine Bob at a country hoedown seeing a pretty girl standing on her own across the room, asking her to dance and reckoning she'll be the one for him. But while lightweight, it is a very listenable track.

'Tomorrow is a Long Time'
A remake of the 1963 soft, tender, heartfelt song of yearning for the loss of Suze, never recorded but sung at New York Town Hall. The band version recorded in the *New Morning* sessions was made into an upbeat country number with Bob assuming a hard-edged vocal while the female backing singers wail away to an earworm of a slide guitar riff.

That's it – the end of the album and the end of the sixties – a new platform for the next decade? An emergence from a hiatus? A rekindling of creative juices? Time would tell.

Selected Bootleg Albums

Bob Dylan is probably the most bootlegged artist on the planet. He even bootlegs himself. Back in the days when there was only vinyl, a whole industry sprang up delivering outtakes and live performances that had never officially seen the light of day. Most of this material was smuggled out of the studio and was of extremely dubious quality. This happened to such a huge degree that Bob and his record label began the process of releasing a number of official bootleg albums. For the first time, a number of these rare recordings and live tracks became available in studio quality.

It would not be possible to review every track and provide detailed information. There are an incredible number of albums and tracks. The book would be much too long. Neither would it be appropriate to deal with these in order of their chronological release dates. I have decided that it is best to select the most important albums based upon the quality of the material or their historical importance.

The Official Bootlegs

These were released in a series titled 'The Bootleg Series'. They had the blessing of both Bob Dylan and his label and were official in every sense. Bob had become completely infuriated with every single outtake, alternative recording, informal taping and live performance being leaked and heavily bootlegged. In an attempt to be in control (and gain some financial recompense), they put together a three-CD official release of a variety of outtakes and other recordings. The official bootleg series was born. They soon realised they were sitting on a gold mine and it spawned a lucrative series (sixteen so far) in which every rehearsal tape, studio outtake, live performance and Dylan fart was examined for release. No tape was left unspun.

The Bootleg Series – Volumes 1-3
Vol. 1

Volume 1 consisted mainly of outtakes from *Bob Dylan*, *Freewheelin'* and *The Times They Are A-Changin'* along with some of the Witmark demos, one home taping and a handful of live tracks from The Gaslight Club, Carnegie Hall and New York Town Hall. It was fabulous to have pristine copies of these tracks after only hearing muddy unofficial bootlegs. There were some brilliant songs officially blasting out of stereo systems for the first time.

Vol. 2

Continued in the same vein with outtakes and alternative versions from *The Times They Are A-Changin'*, *Another Side of Bob Dylan*, *Bringing it All Back Home*, *Highway 61 Revisited*, *Blonde on Blonde*, *The Basement Tapes*, *New Morning*, *Blood on the Tracks* and *Planet Waves*. The wonders continued.

125

The Bootleg Series Vol. 4
The fourth volume saw the release of the full live 1966 Royal Albert Hall concert from May 17th in all its loud, raucous glory.

The Bootleg Series Vol. 6
The 1964 Halloween New York Philharmonic Hall concert in all its glory on a double CD. This is Bob at his best with all those incredible early topical songs and four duets with Joan Baez.

The Bootleg Series Vol. 7: No Direction Home
The soundtrack to the fabulous Martin Scorsese PBS TV documentary *No Direction Home*.

A double CD containing a great array of material spanning 1959 to 1966 with home recordings, party recordings, live material, Witmark demos, TV and alternative takes.

Of particular interest were three exceedingly rare tracks: 'When I Got Troubles' recorded in 1959 by his high school friend Ric Kangas; 'Rambler, Gambler' another home recording from 1960 made by his friend Cleve Petterson; 'This Land is Your Land' a rare recording of a Woody Guthrie song from 1961.

The Bootleg Series Vol. 9: The Witmark Demos: 1962-1964
A double CD containing all the publishing demos for Leeds and Witmark that Dylan recorded between 1962 and 1964. This is Bob with his guitar and harmonica laying down rough and ready versions of his songs in the studio for the publisher to hawk around to other performers. They include versions of some of his best-known songs from that period as well as fifteen songs that he never recorded.

The Bootleg Series Vol. 10: Another Self Portrait: 1969-71
This is a double CD of outtakes, alternative recordings and demos from *Self Portrait*, one of his weakest albums. I think the original was quite enough but in case anybody wants more, the deluxe version runs to four CDs with the whole live at the Isle of Wight and a remastered version of the original album.

The Bootleg Series Vol. 11: The Basement Tapes Complete
A six-CD set of all the unreleased recordings of the basement tapes made in Big Pink and Bob's home. These recordings were made for fun and never intended for official release. There are a number of original Dylan tracks and many traditional songs, making up 138 tracks in total, 117 of which had been previously unreleased.

This pretty much puts to bed the five-CD and four-CD unofficial bootlegged versions of the tapes that came out as *A Tree With Roots* or *The Genuine Bootleg Tapes* with their 128 tracks.

The Bootleg Series Vol. 12: The Cutting Edge 1965-1966
A double CD set of rehearsals, solo acoustic and alternative takes from what is considered to be the absolute pinnacle of Bob's creativity – the albums *Bringing it All Back Home*, *Highway 61 Revisited* and *Blonde on Blonde*.

These will make your brain explode. For those who want more of this magnificent set, there is a four-CD deluxe version. For the completists who won't be satisfied until they have every last note, there is an exhaustive eighteen-CD collector's set which will send you senseless with multiple versions and takes until your brain freezes. There is only so much brilliance that the brain can cope with. The repetition is just too much of a good thing for most people.

The Bootleg Series Vol. 15: Travelin' Thru, 1967-1969
A triple CD collection of alternative versions, outtakes and rehearsals for *John Wesley Harding* and *Nashville Skyline,* along with rehearsals for TV appearances on *The Johnny Cash Show* and the TV special *Earl Scruggs, His Family and Friends*.

Live 1961-2000 – Thirty-Nine Years of Great Concert Performances
A strange eclectic assortment of rare tracks and live performances from the Minneapolis Hotel in 1961 through to concert tracks from 2000.

Live at the Gaslight 1962
Ten of the seventeen tracks recorded at this crossroads concert that bridges between the folk/blues singer of the debut album and the singer/songwriter of the second. For some inexplicable reason, it misses out seven other tracks that have been unofficially available on numerous other bootlegs.

Live at Carnegie Hall 1963
Just six tracks – 32 minutes from the Carnegie Hall concert promoting the *Times They Are A-Changin'* album. Great version of 'Lay Down Your Weary Tune' though.

In Concert – Brandeis University 1963
An interesting, though short, newly discovered concert. A reasonable recording that shows Bob's humour and expressive delivery prior to the release of *Freewheelin'*.

The 1966 Live Recordings
Personnel:
Bob Dylan: acoustic guitar, electric guitar, harmonica, piano, lead vocal
Robbie Robertson: lead guitar
Rick Danko: bass and vocal
Garth Hudson: organ

Richard Manuel: piano
Mickey Jones: drums
Sandy Konikoff: drums (prior to March 26th)
Jeff Rosen: producer
Steve Berkowitz: producer
Label: Columbia records
Recorded between 5 February and 27 May 1966.
Live recording through the soundboard
Release date: November 2016
Highest chart positions: -

A comprehensive collection of all the live recordings on the 1966 tour gathered together in a staggering 36 CD collection. Most are soundboard recordings, but where there was one missing, the best audience recordings have been used. The smorgasbord of delights includes the full concerts from Cardiff, London, Liverpool, Paris, Birmingham, Leicester, Sydney, Melbourne, Copenhagen, Dublin, Belfast, Bristol, Sheffield, Glasgow, Edinburgh, Newcastle, White Plains, Pittsburgh, Hempstead, Stockholm and Manchester.

This is a historic record of the shifting of tectonic plates. You can hear them grinding as the audience struggles to absorb the kaleidoscopic changing of musical masses as they slide across each other, shrieking with the release of energy and causing shockwaves that are still resounding today.

Elvis, Little Richard and The Beatles collide with Allen Ginsberg, Robert Johnson, Woody Guthrie, Rimbaud and LSD. The result is a new wild mercury sound – heavy, volatile and dangerous. Some of the audience groove on it; some are repelled. Not only have they got to get used to a new, loud, raw sound, but they also have to struggle with this new surreal poetry. The clear-cut, finger-pointing lyrics of social justice, civil rights and anti-war that they loved had been replaced by more obscure pictures of abstract weirdness. How could they understand and interpret this? What did it mean?

While many in the audience no doubt felt passionately that Bob was selling out by going electric, felt betrayed and fervently wanted their old Bob back, the protests at the concerts were organised in advance and contrived. It had become a fashion. They were hitching on to a trend. They came along to boo. However, many other sectors of the audience came to listen and were really digging the direction Dylan was going in. Never had an audience been split so profoundly. Mind you, 36 CDs from 21 gigs of Dylan and The Band playing exactly the same set requires a devout, maybe obsessive, love of Dylan and a great ability to focus and concentrate.

The Basement Tapes

These were recorded in 1967 in Bob Dylan's house and the basement of The Band's house – Big Pink in Woodstock. Some 24 tracks were officially released, with overdubs, in 1975 on the double album called *The Basement Tapes*.

The nature of the recordings is markedly different to anything Dylan has done before and is a distinct move away from the mercury sound that preceded them. The original songs are simpler, lack the complex, surreal poetry and have a relaxed upbeat, carefree feel to them. The pressure is off. The sessions are full of joy. There are no frills as Bob and The Band mess about, jamming for fun.

The content contains a lot of covers that range from traditional folk, through to country, r&b, blues and pop. There were songs by Johnny Cash, Hank Williams, Elvis Presley, The Impressions and John Lee Hooker. The Band went on to produce an album based around this style called *Music from Big Pink* and the style became known as Americana, heralding a move away from the heavy psychedelic sound of the sixties to a country-based sound in the seventies.

The 50th Anniversary Collection: The Copyright Extension Collection, Volume 1
After 60 years, recordings enter into the public domain in Europe. In order to prevent this from happening to material recorded by Dylan during 1962, Sony released four CDs of Bob's 1962 material, including rare and unreleased tracks. Before anybody gets too excited, they only released 100 copies and then took them off the market.

These include two CDs of *Freewheelin'* outtakes, The Mackenzie Home tapes, live sets from Gerdes Folk City, the Finjan club, Carnegie Hall and The Gaslight.

The Unofficial Bootlegs
These were recorded by bootleggers, many of whom were merely after making a profit for themselves. Often the equipment used was substandard and the quality of the 'product' inferior. Some of the original material was recorded on reel-to-reel tape machines in friends' homes, in Folk Clubs or at parties. Some were taken from soundboards or PA systems and were very good quality. Not that we, the dyed-in-the-wool Dylan fanatics, cared even if the recordings were poor. We were just grateful to get our hands on fabulous unreleased material. A global network of bootleg exchanges and swaps was established. Magazines sprang up devoted to these bootlegs, discussing songs, recording details and quality. There was a whole multifaceted Bob Dylan bootleg industry.

With the advent of first tapes, then CDs and finally digital, this body of elicit recordings reached epic proportions. It now seems that no performance, no alternative take or unreleased track, is free from being bootlegged.

Many of these bootleg albums are historical documents revealing much about the repertoire, current style and state of mind of Bob throughout the many stages of his incredible career. They are not only great to listen to but provide insight into his musical development.

The John Bucklen Tapes – 1958

These are the earliest recordings we have of Bob Dylan recorded on a reel-to-reel tape recorder. This muddy recording has a seventeen-year-old Bob messing around on piano and guitar and talking with his best friend John Bucklen. The tape features them singing five rock 'n' roll/r&b songs, one of which, 'Little Richard', was a Bob Dylan original. The five songs are 'Little Richard', 'Buzz Buzz Buzz' (Hollywood Flames), 'Jenny Jenny' (Little Richard), 'We Belong Together' (Robert and Johnny) and 'Betty Lou' (sometimes listed as 'Blue Moon')

Interesting to hear the pair of them discuss rock 'n' roll and r&b, with Bob accusing Johnny Cash of being boring.

I Was So Much Younger Then – Vol 1-4 – 1958-1965

This is a remarkable four-CD set that gathers all the early recordings together from numerous other bootlegs. Many of these were recorded on reel-to-reel tape recorders, sometimes at informal gatherings at friends' houses, and hence the recordings are sometimes dismal, but as historical documents, showing how Bob developed during these five seminal years, they are incredible.

We see Bob starting off in Hibbing as a rock 'n' roller in 1958. In Minnesota in 1960, we find him as an acoustic folk singer, covering traditional folk songs, a lot of Woody Guthrie and some acoustic blues. By 1962 in New York, he has already started to write his own material. By the time we get to the 1963-1965 material, we find the fully-fledged Dylan with the complex poetic songs that made his name.

This might not be a set of CDs you'd choose to listen to for pleasure too often because of the quality, but as historical recordings, they are fascinating. For hardened Dylan followers, many of the performances are well worth a spin. There is the chance to hear how Bob tackles the many Guthrie songs in his repertoire in those early days – as these were never properly recorded – an important stage in his development. Bob was not happy about much of this material, feeling that the quality of the recording did not do him justice.

Disc 1

John Bucklen Tape, Hibbing, MN c.1958
Minnesota Party Tape, Minneapolis, Sept 1960
Gerdes Folk City, NY, 29 Sept 1961
Billy James Interview, NY, CBS tape, Nov 1961
Cynthia Gooding, NY, apt. tape, Feb/March 1962
Madhouse on Castle Street, London, 30 Dec 1962

Disc 2

Karen Wallace Tapes, St. Paul, MN, May 1960

Disc 3
Recorded at the NY home of Eve and Mac McKenzie
1st McKenzie Tape, 23 November 1961 and 4 December 1961
2nd McKenzie Tape, 12 April 1963

Disc 4
Indian Neck Folk Festival, Branford, CT, 6 May 1961
Oscar Brand Festival WNYC, NY, 29 October 1961
Oscar Brand Show WNYC, NY, March 1963
Steve Allen TV show LA, CA, 25 February 1964
Les Crane Show WABC-TV, NY, 17 February 1965

The Dylan Apartment Tapes – September 1960
These feature a couple of Woody Guthrie covers 'Jesus Christ' and 'Talkin'
Columbia', a number of folk covers and three other talking blues tracks:
'Talkin' Merchant Marine', 'Talkin' Hugh Brown' and 'Talkin' Inflation
Blues'.

The Minnesota Tapes – May 1961 (Bonnie Beecher Tapes)
Recorded by Bonnie Beecher in her apartment – a young Bob Dylan was
eager to hear the sound of his own voice so that he could develop his style.
The quality of the recordings is poor, but it is interesting to hear the material
that Bob is starting to get to grips with – traditional folk, Woody Guthrie
and some folk blues. The performance is hesitant, but it serves as a great
comparison with other recordings to see how quickly Bob develops. These
are the songs he was using to play in the Minnesota coffee houses in order to
earn a living.

The Minnesota Hotel Tapes (Glover Tapes) – December 1961 –
The Great White Wonder
Just six months later, a more confident Dylan, with a sharper, more focused
performance, can be heard. These recordings were of a higher quality and
when Dylan became a major player, they were seized upon by bootleggers
who put them out as a double vinyl album under the title – *The Great White
Wonder*. They have appeared under various other names ever since. The
material is similar to the earlier tape but with more blues numbers and a
harder edge.

East Orange Tape – Feb-March 1961 (The Gleason Tapes)
These songs were recorded on a reel-to-reel tape recorder in the home of
Bob and Sid Gleason. While the quality is not great, it is more than passable.
The ten songs recorded feature what one would expect from this time – a
number of Woody Guthrie tunes, a couple of folk songs, a Jesse Fuller track
and a Jimmie Rodgers track.

Indian Neck Folk Festival – May 1961

The Indian Neck Folk Festival was a rumbustious gathering at the Montowesi Hotel in Branford Connecticut. There are four poor-quality recordings of Bob playing Woody Guthrie songs along with Mark Spoeltra. It was at this festival that he met up with Bob Neuwirth. It documents how Bob was trying to break into the wider scene and meet and feed off the other performers. Much jamming took place in informal settings around the festival as various singers met up, played together and shared their songs.

Karen Wallace Tapes – May 1961

Karen was an early fan of the emerging Dylan, who was plying his trade around the coffee houses of Minnesota. She set about recording him in her house on a reel-to-reel tape recorder. The result was an hour's recording consisting of some 36 songs, many of which are excerpts, including a number of Woody Guthrie tunes and traditional folk songs. The recordings are reasonable quality though fragmented and chaotic at times.

Riverside Church – July 1961

This was Bob's first radio appearance. He appeared as part of a folk hootenanny that went out on WRVR-FM radio. The show was a rushed amateurish affair and Bob was not too well prepared. He sang five songs (none of his own) and hammed it up in his best Chaplin-esque manner while messing around with a homemade harmonica holder, concocted out of a coat hanger, and using a knife as a slide on his guitar. His final song was a mess around comical duet with Ramblin' Jack Elliott. The quality is good even if the material wasn't stunning, but it all seemed to go down well.

The Carnegie Chapter Hall – November 1961

This was the first time Bob had ventured out of the coffee houses into a more formal concert setting and, as such, is a real historic event. The recordings were from the PA but are far from perfect. The material features Woody Guthrie, Leadbelly, Bessie Smith and Blind Lemon Jefferson covers as well as traditional folk songs. There were no Dylan originals.

McKenzie Tapes – 1961-1962

Soon after arriving in New York, Bob was introduced to Eve and Mac McKenzie by none other than Woody Guthrie's wife Majorie. The couple had an apartment near the Village which became a haunt of many of the up-and-coming folk singers. Bob was a regular and spent many a night sleeping on their couch. Over the course of two years, between 1961 and 1962, they made a number of primitive home recordings. 30 of these tracks were released as a bootleg. They contained a range of folk, blues, Hank Williams, Jesse Fuller and Woody Guthrie numbers as well as the odd original. As one might expect, the later recordings featured more Dylan numbers – 'Hard

Times in New York Town', 'The Death of Emmitt Till', 'A Hard Rain's a-Gonna Fall' and 'Ballad of Donald White'.

Blind Boy Grunt – 1961-1962

Blind Boy Grunt was the alias Bob adopted in order to avoid any contractual infringement with his recordings for Colombia while laying down some tracks for the Folkways *Broadside* magazine. He recorded three tracks for them under the epithet of Blind Boy Grunt – 'John Brown', 'Only a Hobo' and 'Talkin' Devil'. The strange name came about when he couldn't remember a verse and was told to grunt instead. The name is a humorous play on the names of some of the old blues singers. It was an alias that he also used when he added harmonica and backing to an album by Richard Farina and Eric Von Schmidt.

Blind Boy Grunt was used on a number of bootleg albums, such as the double album *Blind Boy Grunt* which was mainly a rehash of the Minnesota tapes along with the two Broadside tracks, plus a track from the 1961 WBAI radio track – 'The Ballad of Donald White'.

Those three Broadside tracks were released on the album *Broadside Ballads*. A few more Dylan Broadside songs were later released on the Folkways *Broadside Reunion* album.

Echo's Album – 1961-1963

Echo Helstrom was an important early girlfriend of Bob's in Hibbing. They dated for a year when Bob was in school. She was a wild character and had an impact on his musical development, both of them listening to rock and r&b, and her father's folk collection. She is thought to be the muse for a number of Bob's songs.

This double album bootleg gathered together a number of disparate sources and is good quality:

New York Riverside Church – July 1961
Gerde's Folk City – May 1962
Quest TV Show – February 1964
The Bear, Chicago – May 1963
Skip Weshner Show – February 1963
Billy Faier Show – October 1962
British TV, Dilworth – May 1964
Songs of Freedom WNEW-TV – July 1963

The Gaslight Tapes – September 1961-October 1962

There were three separate concerts although they have been released in various forms and muddled together so that the actual running order of the songs is hard to determine. As they were recorded through the house PA, the quality is brilliant. Tape one, recorded in September 1961, is the first known concert recording of Bob's and features six songs, three of which are Dylan originals: 'Man on the Street', 'Talkin' Bear Mountain Picnic Massacre Blues' and 'Song to Woody'. The second tape is from October 1962, and features ten songs with two originals: 'John Brown' and 'The Ballads of Hollis Brown'. The third tape was a concert from around the same time as the second. It featured seven songs with two Dylan originals: 'Don't Think Twice it's Alright' and 'A Hard Rain's a-Gonna Fall'.

As Bob released his first album in March 1962 and was recording his second album in May 1963, these concerts are great insights into the material he was performing and writing at that time.

For Sale or Just on the Shelf – Vol 1-6 – 1961-1964

A stunning six-CD collection of outtakes, alternative mixes and live performances of exceptional quality. The collection brought together a large number of rare and well-recorded songs from early on in Dylan's career, many of which could easily have featured on the albums and some of which were among his best songs. Some were left off albums for political reasons, others because it felt that they were too similar to included tracks or simply did not fit in with the ambience of the album. A number were left out because Bob had simply moved on to a different sound before they could be released. There is a wealth of brilliant early songs:

Vol 1 – Colombia Records outtakes 1961-1962
Vol 2 – Colombia Records outtakes 1962
Vol 3 – Alternative mixes – 1963
Vol 4 – Alternative mixes – 1964
Vol 5 – Live versions of outtakes
Vol 6 – Live versions of outtakes

In the Pines – November 1961 – March 1965

This superb album takes its name from the first track – a cover of the Leadbelly number recorded in 1961 at the Carnegie Hall concert. It then continues with another Carnegie Hall track and proceeds through the music from the Chicago Bear Club in 1963, which unfortunately, has been edited to remove all the banter between songs in order to fit them all in. However, the main feature of the album lies in the tremendous remastering of the eleven Leeds publishing demos recorded between 1962 and 1965. There are some absolute gems.

Folksinger's Choice – Cynthia Gooding radio show – February 1962

Cynthia Gooding was a folk singer who hosted a popular folk music programme on New York WBIA radio station. She was highly thought of and provided a springboard for new folk talent to get noticed. In 1962, shortly before the release of his debut album, Bob appeared on the show and produced a relaxed performance in which he sang and talked about his career. The quality is fabulous, the songs great, even though they are mainly the folk blues covers he was playing at the time with just two originals, and the conversation between the tracks is priceless. This is a fabulous insight into Bob's thinking prior to him being known outside the small bubble of New York's Greenwich Village. The two Dylan songs to get an outing are 'The Death of Emmitt Till' and 'Hard Time in New York'.

Cynthia Gooding's Apartment Tapes – 1962

Cynthia used to entertain aspiring folk singers in her apartment. Bob was one of them and we are fortunate enough to have some good-quality recordings that she made from this time. There are six recordings on this tape, including 'The Ballad of Donald White'.

Gerdes Folk City – April 1962

A concert at Gerdes Folk City on 16 April 1962 has been widely bootlegged with songs appearing on a number of unofficial albums, including *Paranoid Blues* and *Bob Dylan's Dream Vol 2*. The tracks used were 'Honey Just Allow Me One More Chance', 'Talkin' New York /Talkin' Folk Lore' Center', 'Corrina Corrina', 'Deep Ellum Blues' and 'Blowin' in the Wind'. The quality is good and there are probably more to come from the same source.

The Finjan Club Montreal – 2 July 1962

By July 1962, Albert Grossman was beginning to get Bob gigs out of town in order to increase his profile. One of these jaunts was to Montreal in Canada, where he produced a blistering set. Fortunately for us, the set was recorded through the soundboard and we have a pristine 1962 Bob Dylan gig in all its glory.

What is interesting to see is that Bob is singing blues songs by Robert Johnson, Muddy Waters and Brownie McGhee, the Memphis Jugband's 'Stealin'', some traditional folk songs, a Jimmie Rodgers number and now interspersing his own songs of social commentary like 'The Death of Emmitt Till', 'Blowin' in the Wind' and 'Let Me Die in My Footsteps'. By this time, half of the songs were originals. The poetic beast was beginning to emerge.

Through a Bullet of Light – July 1962-March 1964

These are 41 of the Witmark demos recorded for the publishing company so that they could be touted to other artists – therefore, they are not the finished article. These recordings are raw and simple with just Bob, his guitar and his harmonica. They highlight Bob's songwriting abilities and demonstrate a frightening array of brilliant songs all written within a very short time period. These tracks are basic but brilliant.

Banjo Tape NYC – Gerdes Folk City – February 1963

This was given the title among bootleggers because Happy Traum was playing banjo and providing backing vocals (Gill Turner providing backing vocals on the last track). For a long time, it was thought to have been a home recording, but that proved not to be the case. It features Dylan originals in the form of 'Masters of War' and 'Bob Dylan's Dream' as well as a Leadbelly number, some traditional songs and the Memphis Jugband favourite 'Stealin''.

Studs Terkel's Wax Museum – May 1963
Studs Terkel was a giant of a character, a fearless writer and radio presenter who was proudly blacklisted during the red scare of the McCarthy era. He gave thousands of interviews to record an oral history of America. On 1 May 1963, this behemoth turned his attention to the emerging genius of the social phenomenon that was Bob Dylan.

Blowing into Chicago to make his appearance on Studs' prestigious showcase radio show – The Wax Museum – we find Bob on the cusp of great change. Full of bite and wit, he articulately launches himself into a new era. His second album, *Freewheelin'*, is in the can and due to be released in a couple of weeks. This new Dylan is fiery with social rhetoric and poetic songs that reflect this stance. He was taking Woody's songs a stage further and is poised to take things to a new level. Studs' show is a great platform with which to launch this new tempest of a performer.

Bob's performance is now firmly based on all his own songs and he is taking no prisoners. No topic is off his agenda as he attacks the capitalist system that creates war and inequality. The standard of recording is excellent. The conversation and performance superb. This is the seminal Dylan at the beginning of his purple patch. Studs gives him the launchpad. Bob seizes the moment. This is a diamond of a show that always brings a big grin to my face. This is the start.

The contents of the show display just how far Bob has come in such a short period of time: 'Farewell', 'Hard Rain', 'Bob Dylan's Dream', 'Boots of Spanish Leather', 'John Brown', 'Who Killed Davey Moore?' and 'Blowin' in the Wind' all demonstrate the wide range of the content that make up the new lexicon.

New York Town Hall – April 1963
This concert was properly recorded from the soundboard with a view to releasing a live album that never happened. The performance consisted of all Bob Dylan songs – 'Bob Dylan's Dream', 'Tomorrow is a Long Time', 'Bob Dylan's New Orleans Rag', 'Masters of War', 'Walls of Red Wing', 'Hero Blues', 'Who Killed Davey Moore?', 'With God on Our Side ', 'Last Thoughts on Woody Guthrie', 'Dusty Old Fairgrounds', 'All Over You' and 'John Brown', apart from an adaptation of a Woody Guthrie song – 'Ramblin' Through the World'.

Because of its quality and the performances of some quite rare Dylan originals, this was a much sought-after bootleg.

Bob Fass Radio Show – March 1963

Bob, clutching an early acetate of his shortly-to-be-released *Freewheelin'* album, accompanied by Suze Rotolo, invades the WBAI-FM radio station to brazenly promote the new album. Most of the show is not about Bob and his music. The rest is made up of some tracks off the new acetate – no tracks are played that are different to what eventually comes out on the *Freewheelin'* album and tracks that later get switched from the album do not feature. There is some joking around between Bob and Suze; this is the only time we get to hear Bob and Suze together.

Bear Club Chicago – April 1963

A great-sounding concert, brilliantly recorded and featuring the burgeoning Dylan at his best. He was hot. This reflects the power of these new songs – songs like 'A Hard Rain's a-Gonna Fall', 'Ballad of Hollis Brown' and 'With God on Our Side' added a different dimension and dynamic. You could hear that Bob was heading into hyperdrive. Songs like 'Talkin' John Birch Paranoid Blues', 'Talkin' World War III Blues' and 'Bob Dylan's Dream' balanced the act with killer humour whilst still dealing with social themes. This was the lift-off of a phenomenon.

The March On Washington – 28 August 1963

The young Bob Dylan had hit the stratosphere and his topical songs had not only propelled him to the brink of international fame but 'married' him to Joan Baez as the King and Queen of folk. When 200,000 people marched to the Lincoln Memorial to protest racial discrimination and demand equal rights, they went to hear Martin Luther King deliver his rousing 'I Have a Dream' speech. They were also roused by Bob's songs of firebrand fury. *Freewheelin'* had propelled him to the fore as a major player in the realm of civil rights. A blinking Bob Dylan gave a faultless performance of 'When the Ship Comes In' and 'Only a Pawn in Their Game' amply backed by Joan on harmonies, while Peter, Paul and Mary delivered their big hit of Dylan's anthem 'Blowin' in the Wind'.

Twelve Curses – 1963

Bob was a whirlwind of creativity. He was riding the beast. Songs were flying out of his pen and guitar at an astounding rate. Not just any songs, but brilliant songs of depth and value. Hot on the heels of the breakthrough *Freewheelin'*, Bob was in the studio recording the next album. As with *Freewheelin'*, there were many more songs than could possibly fit on the album. Many great songs were left in the can. Some were left off because their tone did not fit the sombre, message fuelled atmosphere, others were simply left behind in the dust, superseded by newer songs.

Twelve Curses was, in its day, a glorious cornucopia of eleven great outtakes from the new *The Times They Are A-Changin'* album. As these tracks have now all found their way, in better quality, onto official releases, the importance of the album has greatly diminished.

Philharmonic Hall New York – October 1964

This concert first appeared as a bootleg entitled *All Hallow's Eve and More*. It went on to appear in many guises under a variety of names until eventually finding an official release. The concert clearly reveals how fast Bob was developing as a songwriter and the prodigious flow of stellar new material. It was a showcase for new gems such as 'It's Alright Ma, I'm Only Bleeding', 'To Ramona', 'Spanish Harlem Incident' and 'The Gates of Eden'.

Emmet Grogan Acetates – June 1964

Emmet Grogan was the founder of the Californian Diggers: a radical group of social activists who took their name from the English Diggers of the seventeenth century.

These tapes were unreleased demos of excellent quality. The two standout tracks being the original demo of 'Mr Tambourine Man' performed as a duet with Ramblin' Jack Elliott (the version that was sent to The Byrds) and a version of 'All I Really Want to Do' with an extra verse.

San Jose – November 1964

A lousy audience-generated recording of the concert that sounds distant, tinny and pretty crap but is renowned for having the very last performance of 'Talkin' John Birch Paranoid Blues' and the last outing of 'A Hard Rain's a-Gonna Fall' for seven years. Bob was riding the cusp of change and this was a watershed.

Free Wheelin' Sessions

This bootleg is brilliant – sharp and clear right off the studio mixing desk. The material is superb and shows exactly where Bob's head was at during these sessions. At first, there are still the old blues covers as with 'Baby Please Don't Go', 'Milk Cow's Calf's Blues' and 'That's Alright Mama' and the folk covers with 'Corina Corina' and 'Lonesome Whistle'; the kind of material that Bob had been playing in the clubs and had featured on the debut album. But there were also the new, original compositions, the type of stuff that was going to feature on *Freewheelin'* and *The Times They Are A-Changin'*. It is fascinating to hear the tracks left off the album, such as the stellar 'Talkin' John Birch Paranoid Blues ', 'Let Me Die in My Footsteps' and 'The Death of Emmett Till'. There is even an early version of 'The Ballad of Hollis Brown' which wouldn't appear until the following album. Then we have the electric experiment of 'Mixed Up Confusion' that shone briefly as a single.

My only criticism is that it's far too short. There are too many brilliant outtakes that are not included. *Freewheelin'* was his most prolifically creative period. It should have been a double album and included every single one of the amazing set of outtakes.

It makes you wonder why Dylan and Colombia didn't bring *Freewheelin'* out as a double album. They certainly had the material.

Witmark Demos – 1963-64

This came out as a double CD with 47 titles. The bootleg has been superseded with an official release as the ninth instalment in Bob's bootleg series.

The tracks, recorded for the Leeds and Witmark publishing houses, are rough demos. They were not recorded for performance but merely to highlight the song and arrangement for other artists to record properly. A number of the tracks were recorded by Bob on various albums but many weren't. The incredible thing is to be able to hear those unrecorded songs – even if they are very rough and ready. It's a shame that the quality of the recording is not a shade better.

Broadside Demos – 1963-1964

The *Broadside* magazine was a magazine that featured topical folk songs. As the name suggests, it was left-wing and vociferous, mimicking the Broadsides of the sixteenth century. It published articles on the singers and the lyrics and music of their songs. Phil Ochs was a major contributor. Bob also contributed during this period. As far as songwriting went, this was Bob's golden period. Songs were falling out of him like a stream of honey from a hive. The magazine also produced albums and recorded their featured artists.

These fourteen tracks were gathered together and released along with a few WBAI radio tracks ('The Ballad of Donald White', 'The Death of Emmett Till' and a version of 'Blowin' in the Wind' with Pete Seeger, Sis Cunningham and Gil Turner) as well as a couple of tracks from the Washington civil rights march ('Only a Pawn in Their Game' and 'Keep Your Eyes on the Prize' with Joan Baez and Len Chandler).

Among these recordings there were a number of very rare Dylan songs: 'I'd Hate to Be You on That Dreadful Day', 'Paths of Victory', 'Walkin' Down the Line', 'Playboys and Playgirls', 'Talkin' Devil', 'Farewell', 'Only a Hobo', 'Train a-Travellin'', and 'Cuban Missile Crisis'.

Newport Folk Festival – 1963-1965

This bootleg CD features all 20 tracks from the Newport festival starting with the acoustic sets from 1963 and 1964, including duets with Pete Seeger and Joan Baez, and culminating with the controversial electric set in 1965 with the Paul Butterworth band.

The quality is not brilliant, but the historic nature of the sets makes it a must. I used to have this on tape and played it to death in the car. That electric performance was scintillating. It catalogued a historic incident that was a monumental watershed.

There is a video release by Murray Lerner, called *The Other Side Of The Mirror*, which covers this as well providing a visual and aural record.

Folk Rogue – 1964-1965
A cracking CD of soundboard material from both the 1964 Newport Festival and that magical electric performance at the 1965 Newport Festival. The three filler tracks are brilliant, too – the two missing tracks from The 1965 Hollywood Bowl and one from Newcastle 1965. I prefer this to the previous album.

1964 Revisited Vol 1-9 – 1964
A nine-CD comprehensive gathering of material from the whole of 1964. It includes outtakes, gigs and demos – Columbia studio outtakes, Witmark demos, Emmet Grogan acetates, Newport Festival live performances, the Philadelphia Town Hall gig, New York Philharmonic Hall gig and San Jose gig.

Thin Wild Mercury Sound – 1965
A virtually pristine set of outtakes from the *Bringing it All Back Home* and *Highway 61 Revisited* sessions. A little jumbled up, but some superb outtakes, early versions and unreleased songs, including 'Jet Pilot', the vitriolic 'She's Your Lover Now' and 'I Wanna Be Your Lover'. This plays as well as any official album and is one that I come back to time and time again.

Lonesome Sparrow Sings – 1965
Another set of pristine soundboard tracks from *Bringing it All Back Home*, *Highway 61 Revisited* and *Blonde on Blonde* sessions. There is quite an overlap with *Thin Wild Mercury Sound,* but there are also some other gems and historical artefacts.

I can't help feeling how much Bob must have hated having everything he'd ever done leaked out to the bootleggers.

Electric Black Nite Crash – 1965
A superb concert from The Hollywood Bowl with an electric backing band. Following the baptism of fire at Newport, where Dylan dipped his toe into the seething cauldron of electricity, Bob was not going to be cowed by the negative reception. He always says that he doesn't respond to pressure or critics; that he always does exactly what he wants. The electricity had entered his veins and lit up his brain. Bob immediately went into the studio and began recording with a range of electric musicians.

In 1965, at the beginning of this exercise, he set about putting a band together to tour. As the Butterfield Blues Band were not available, he searched for a new backing band and found it in The Hawks. The first outing of Robbie Robertson on guitar, Al Kooper on organ, Harvey Brooks on bass and Levon Helm on drums was the first tentative step. Electric Black Nite Crash captured the transition. At The Hollywood Bowl and Forest Hills, Bob was testing the water and searching for the right sound. This new venture, back to that rock 'n' roller from 1958, was giving Bob a new lease of life. He was loving it.

The opening acoustic set is scintillating, deservingly eliciting a positive reaction. For the second set, the band feature. They are not as loud or dynamic as on the later even more controversial 1966 tour, but they were still loud enough to set off a negative reaction within the audience. Here it was – the historic shift – captured in full glory on a superb recording and very listenable too!

Spider's Web – 1965
The bulk of the album is taken from 1965/66 sessions in New York's Colombia Studios: 'It Takes a Lot to Laugh, It Takes a Train to Cry,' 'Positively 4th Street', 'Can You Please Crawl Out Your Window ' (two versions), 'Tombstone Blues', 'Sitting on a Barbed Wire', 'Medicine Sunday', 'I Wanna Be Your Lover', 'Number One' (a rare instrumental outtake from Blonde on Blonde from the Hawks sessions in 1965) , 'She's Your Lover Now' and 'Visions of Johanna'. All in great soundboard quality.

The three Newport 65 tracks were cleaned up a lot and sounded good. A great CD.

The Circus is in Town – 1965 (The BBC Tapes)
On 1 June 1965, Bob recorded a session of twelve songs for the BBC. They were subsequently aired in two halves. There is no soundboard recording, but these tracks released on this bootleg have been recorded from the TV and suffer a little from that. The best versions are to be found on the *1965 Revisited* set. The significance of this pivotal set is that it represents Dylan prior to him entering his electric phase.

Les Crane Show – 1965
In February 1965, Bob appeared for an extensive interview on the Les Crane show in which he gave live performances of two songs – 'It's All Over Now Baby Blue' and 'It's Alright Ma (I'm Only Bleeding)'. They were exemplary recordings that heralded the end of his acoustic phase and appeared on a number of bootlegs, including *I Was So Much Younger Then* and *65 Revisited*.

1965 Revisited – 1965
A brilliant fourteen-CD retrospective of everything that Bob produced in 1965. All the best versions. It includes all the outtakes, live performances and interviews. More than you could ever want.

Manchester Freetrade Hall – 1966 (Now Ain't the Time For Your Tears)
An infamous concert that was greatly bootlegged and wrongly attributed to the Royal Albert Hall.

The first half of the concert was Dylan performing his acoustic set and was warmly received. For the second half, Bob came out and plugged in his electric guitar backed by The Band (formerly The Hawks). As soon as they launched into their electric set, it unleashed a torrent of abuse from a hardcore element of folkies in the audience. Thisis the concert that gave rise to what is probably the most notorious heckle of all time when someone yelled out 'Judas'.

Bob claimed to have been tired of performing the acoustic songs and was even considering getting out of the business. Going electric revitalised his interest. Although he was booed and around a quarter of the audience walked out during the electric set, half of them really liked this new electric version of Dylan. The sales of his electric albums were even higher than the acoustic. In typical Dylan style, Bob took no notice of any criticism and did exactly what he wanted.

People later suggested that a good part of the problem was the sound system which was simply not up to coping with the volume and it was the distorted, incoherent 'noise' that most of the audience were objecting to. That might have been true for some but there was a hardcore element of folkies who regarded folk as cerebral, intellectual and authentic and looked down on rock as low-brow, commercial and distinctly vulgar. I think that snobbery had a large part to play.

For years I played this bootleg; even though the recording was far from perfect, the vibe was as electric as the band. It was only when the concert was released officially in the fabulous 36 CD 1966 Live box set that I was able to hear it from the mixing desk, undistorted, with audible asides in all its glory. What a concert! What a period of time!

While the Establishment Burns – 1966
An intriguing title taken from the name of a Bob Dylan song that has never materialised, probably never even written.

In reality, the album is a mess – an incongruous mix of two concerts from two totally different eras. Side one is from the New York Town Hall concert in 1963 and side two is from Dublin in 1966. They don't have an awful lot in common.

Legend in His Own Time – 1966
A three-CD collection of rarities from sessions and live recordings starting with the Denver Tapes in 1966 and finishing with Ottawa in 1992. The quality is a little variable but generally good. Unfortunately, it is the Denver Tapes that suffer the most.

Jewels and Binoculars – Vols 1-26 – 1966
Wow!! A 26-CD set that attempts to bring together everything that Bob Dylan did in 1966 – from the radio, through live performances to studio sessions.

Quite an undertaking. It's not a set that anyone will find themselves playing all the way through too often, more something to dip in and out of, and much of it has been superseded by the official release of *The 1966 Live Recordings* boxset.

A Tree with Roots

These are the raw, unedited, basement tapes with 108 tracks put out on four CDs. The quality is very good though there is a degree of variability and some of the tracks are fragmentary. There is a lot of repetition on the later CDs with multiple takes of the same song. This bootleg, while capturing the important changes that were taking place in Bob's world, has been superseded by the release of *The Bootleg Series Vol. 11: The Basement Tapes Complete*. This historic document of a new playful Dylan heralds the beginning of a new age of Americana.

Bibliography

Cott, J., *Dylan on Dylan* (Wenner Media LLC, 2006)

Dylan, B., *Chronicles* (Simon & Schuster UK, 2005)

Dylan, B., *Tarantula* (MacGibbon and Kee Ltd, 1971)

Dylan, B., *The Definitive Bob Dylan Songbook* (Music Sales Ltd, 2016)

Gray, M., *Song and Dance Man* (Granada Publishing Ltd, 1972)

Greil, M., *Bob Dylan Writings 1968-2010* (Faber & Faber, 2011)

Heylin, C., *Behind the Shades* (Faber & Faber; Main edition, 2011)

Heylin, C., *Revolution in the Air* (Constable & Robinson Ltd, 2010)

Lee, CP., *Like the Night (Revisited)* (Helter Skelter, 2004)

Rotolo, S., *A Freewheelin' Time* (Aurum Press, 2008)

Scaduto, A., *Bob Dylan* (W. H. Allen and Co Ltd, 1972)

Scaduto, A. & Trudeau, S., *The Dylan Tapes* (University of Minnesota Press, 2021)

Shelton, R., *No Direction Home – The Life and Music of Bob Dylan* (New English Library, 1986)

Sounes, H., *Down the Highway – The Life of Bob Dylan* (Doubleday, 2001)

Spitz, B., *Dylan – A Biography* (W. W. Norton & Company, 1991)

Thompson, T., *Bob Dylan – Positively Main Street* (NEL, 1971)

Internet

Eyolf Østrem – *Dylan Chords* dylanchords.com